DAMMIT!
I SWALLOWED
ANOTHER ONE!

BY KIT LIVELY

Dammit! I Swallowed Another One!

Published in the USA by:

BearManor Media
P.O. Box 71426
Albany, Georgia 31708
www.BearManorMedia.com

ISBN-10: 1-59393-651-6 (alk. paper)
ISBN-13: 978-1-59393-651-8 (alk. paper)

Book design and layout by Valerie Thompson.

TABLE OF CONTENTS

ACKNOWLEDGMENTS

Thanks to my beautiful wife for helping me select the cartoons used in this book; if you don't like the selection, she's partially to blame. Also, thanks to my friends and family for being supportive of my work, even when it's displayed next to photos of naked ladies in uncomfortable-looking poses. Lastly, a big thanks to Scott Nickel, Noel Anderson and Diego Jourdan, my sometime collaborators who hide my crummy ideas behind incredible art (as evidenced by the fact that their artwork is nowhere in this book).

FOREWORD
BY SHANNON WHEELER

Kit Lively has created some of the worst cartoons I have ever read. Most of them are offensive and not very funny. And to make matters worse his drawings are terrible—something a high school senior would do to deface an Algebra book in a class he's failing.

That said, they make me laugh. When he hits with a gag it shoots an arrow to my heart and severs an essential life-tube of aortic blood and he makes me laugh. Embryo-yo is still one of the dumbest jokes I've ever read and also funny as hell. Where the hell did that come from? I'm pissed I didn't think of it. I would never think of it. I could never think of it. It's outside and beyond me and it makes me happy. I'm jealous. Screw him and his stupid jokes. He can't draw. His jokes aren't funny. Then I'm hit again. This time from behind, somewhere between my 7th and 8th vertebrae; something terrible won't let my brain communicate with major parts of my body and I'm laughing again. It's terrible. And it's funny. A lot of his jokes are terrible. A lot of his jokes make me laugh.

Some people like things because they're so bad they're good. You might think that that's what I'm saying. No. Kit's cartoons are good because they're funny. I will punch anyone (except maybe a nun) in the face who argues otherwise. Kit gets to the essence of cartooning. His cartoons contain what they need to carry the joke. He hits in unexpected places and his drawings are perfect for the punch. He doesn't hide behind slick BS like vector computer drawing, rendered coloring, fancy language, cross hatching, abstract humor, tired

Star Trek references or mediocre web cartoon serialized drama with vaguely cute girls. His cartoons hit hard and fast and, usually, below the belt (or spine or heart). They're cartoons, dammit, and Kit is a cartoonist in the honest and truest sense of the word. My hat goes off to him and I wish him luck, even if I am jealous.

Shannon Wheeler
2011

INTRODUCTION
BY JAMES O'BARR

I've known Kit Lively for roughly five years now and he's still a mystery to me. This is what I do know about him:

He likes, no, ADORES bad horror movies, the kind that aren't really scary, just silly with gratuitous nudity. He can recite the entire genealogy of the slasher film, the stars, directors, screen ratios, even the fucking grips. That being said, men are mostly shallow creatures and we all like movies with titties and blood. Kit, however, likes the blood to be on the titties. I am concerned.

Like a true professional he draws his cartoons on notebook paper with Sharpies, no pencils; he just starts with a foot and in mere moments there is a badly drawn gag. Amazing.

He has somehow managed to snag a completely adorable wife, Julie, who, if not wholly appreciating his sense of humor, at least tolerates it.

He snores like a chainsaw badly in need of oiling.

He can somehow draw the most vile cartoons ever with no sarcasm, is never mean spirited, and never at anyone's expense, not an easy feat. Kind of a retarded innocent.

He likes to joke about his small dick, which makes me think maybe it isn't.

He has a lifetime membership to the Mr. Skin website and may even be tenured.

He smokes and drinks too much so he does have some redeeming qualities after all.

He is my good friend, says he loves me in a non-gay way, and, because there is so much crossover potential between sixteen year old Goth girls and *Mad* magazine readers, he asked me to write this introduction. For free.

JAMES O'BARR

CARTOONS

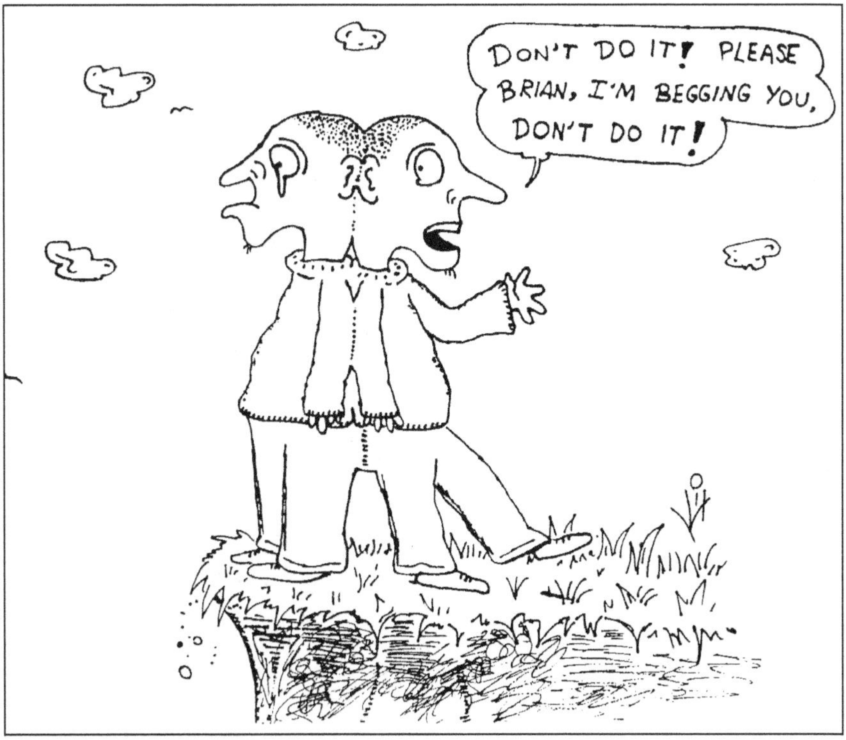
DON'T DO IT! PLEASE BRIAN, I'M BEGGING YOU, DON'T DO IT!

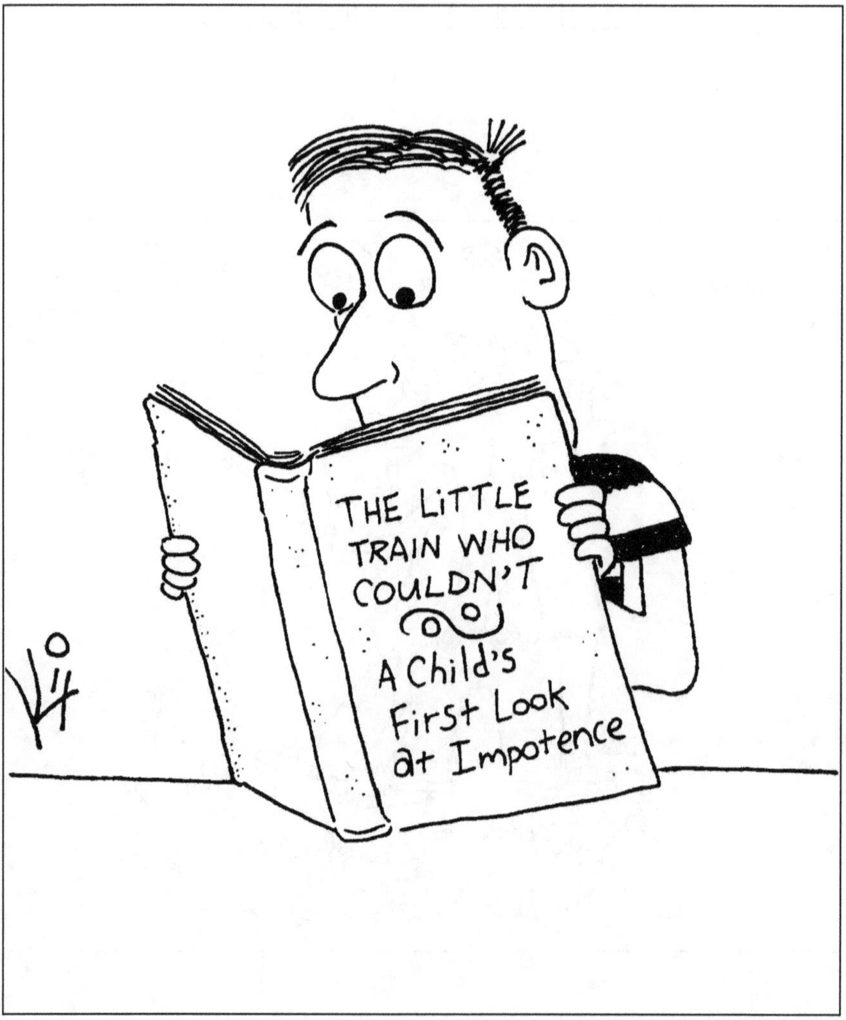
THE LITTLE TRAIN WHO COULDN'T
A Child's First Look at Impotence

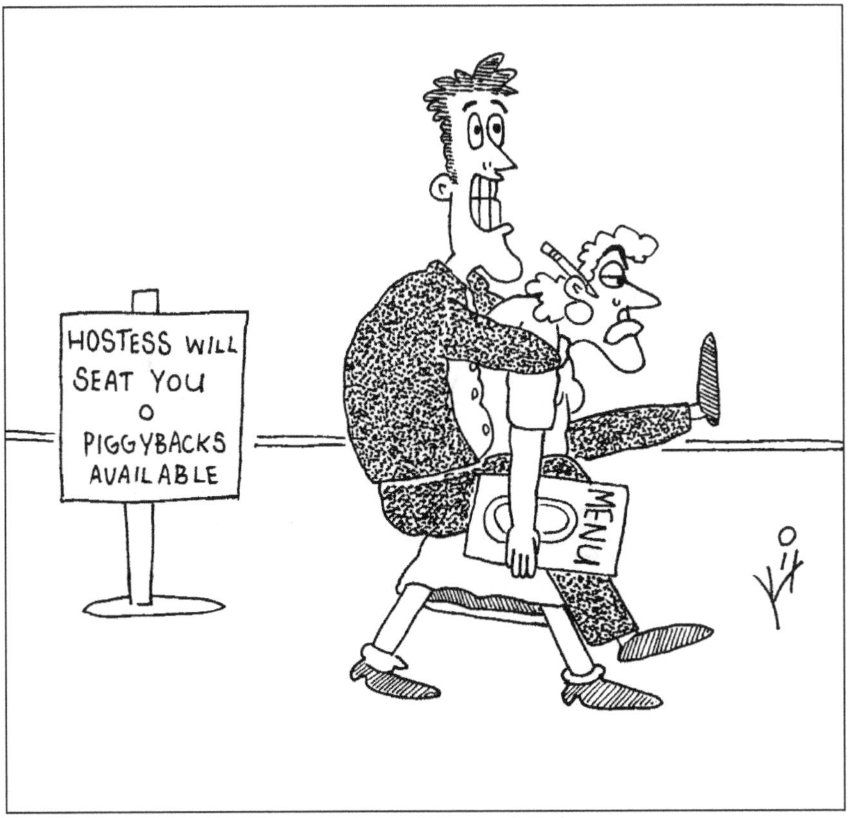
HOSTESS WILL
SEAT YOU
PIGGYBACKS
AVAILABLE
MENU

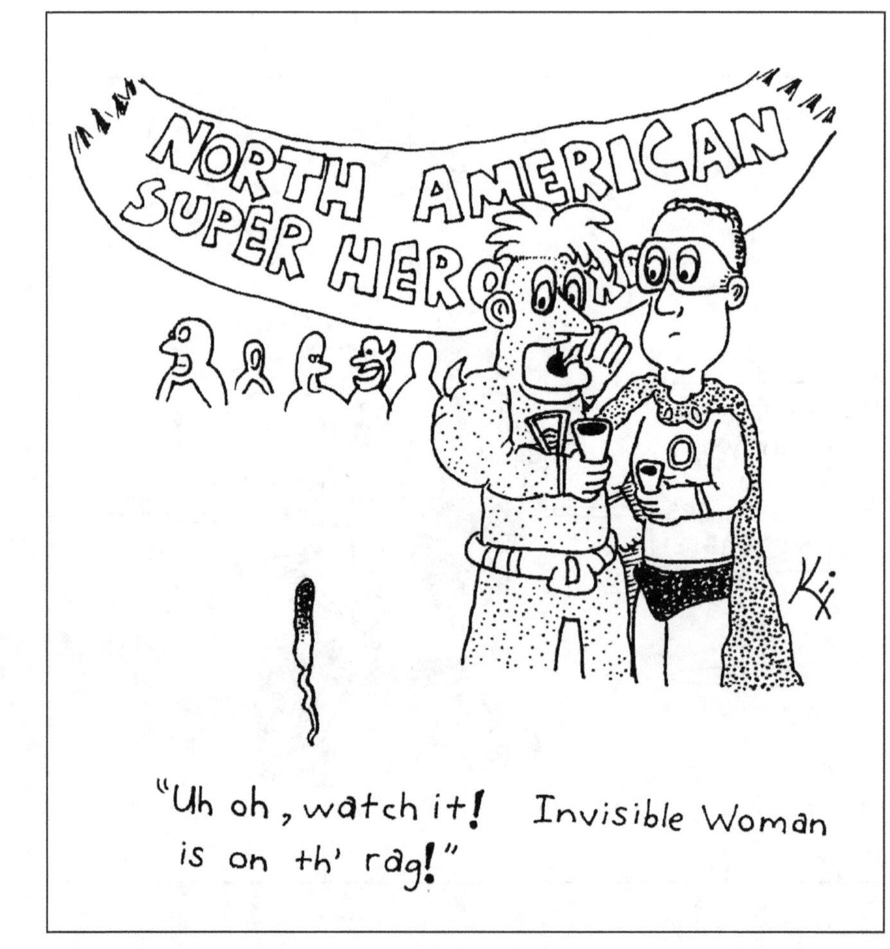
NORTH AMERICAN
SUPER HERO

"Uh oh, watch it! Invisible Woman is on th' rag!"

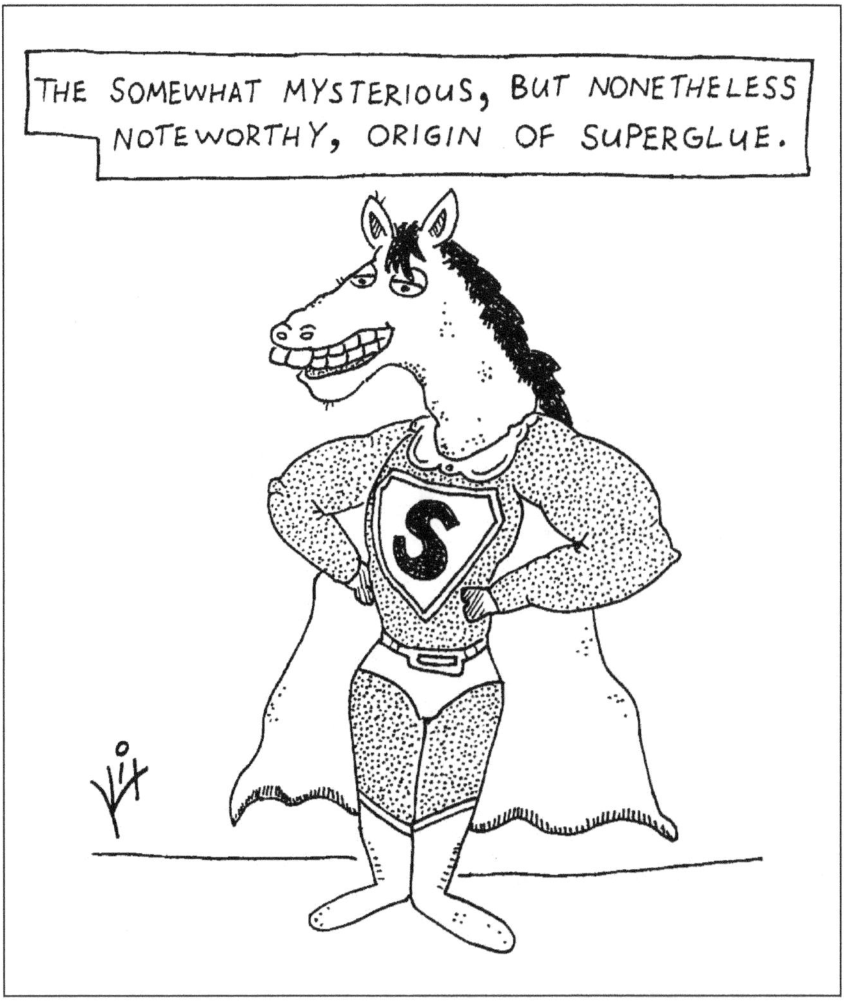
THE SOMEWHAT MYSTERIOUS, BUT NONETHELESS NOTEWORTHY, ORIGIN OF SUPERGLUE.
S

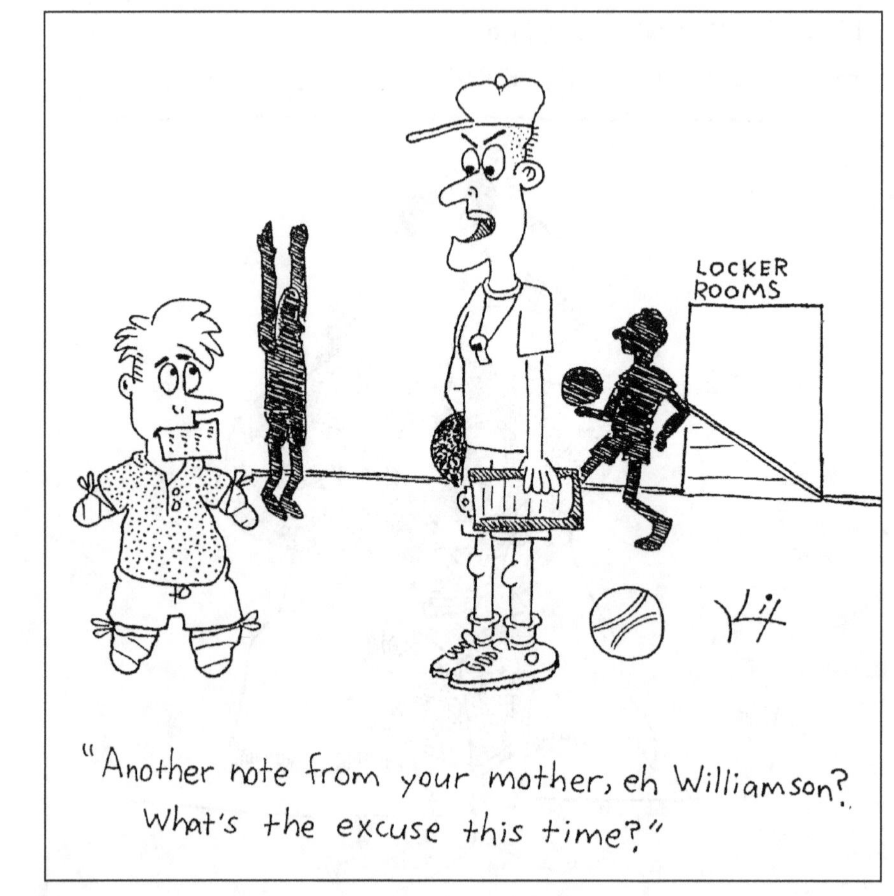
LOCKER
ROOMS

"Another note from your mother, eh Williamson? What's the excuse this time?"

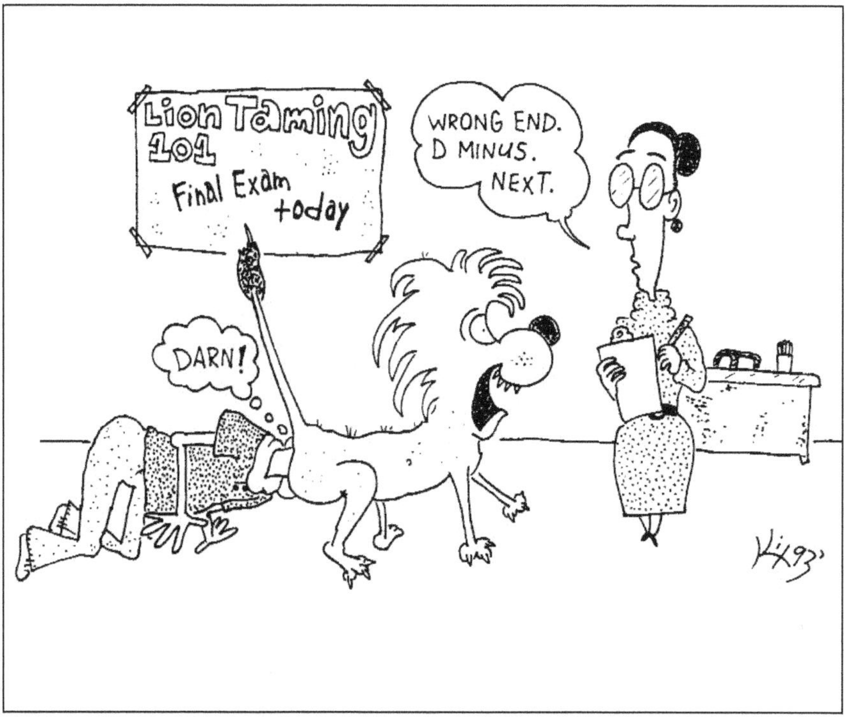
Lion Taming 101
Final Exam today
WRONG END. D MINUS. NEXT.
DARN!

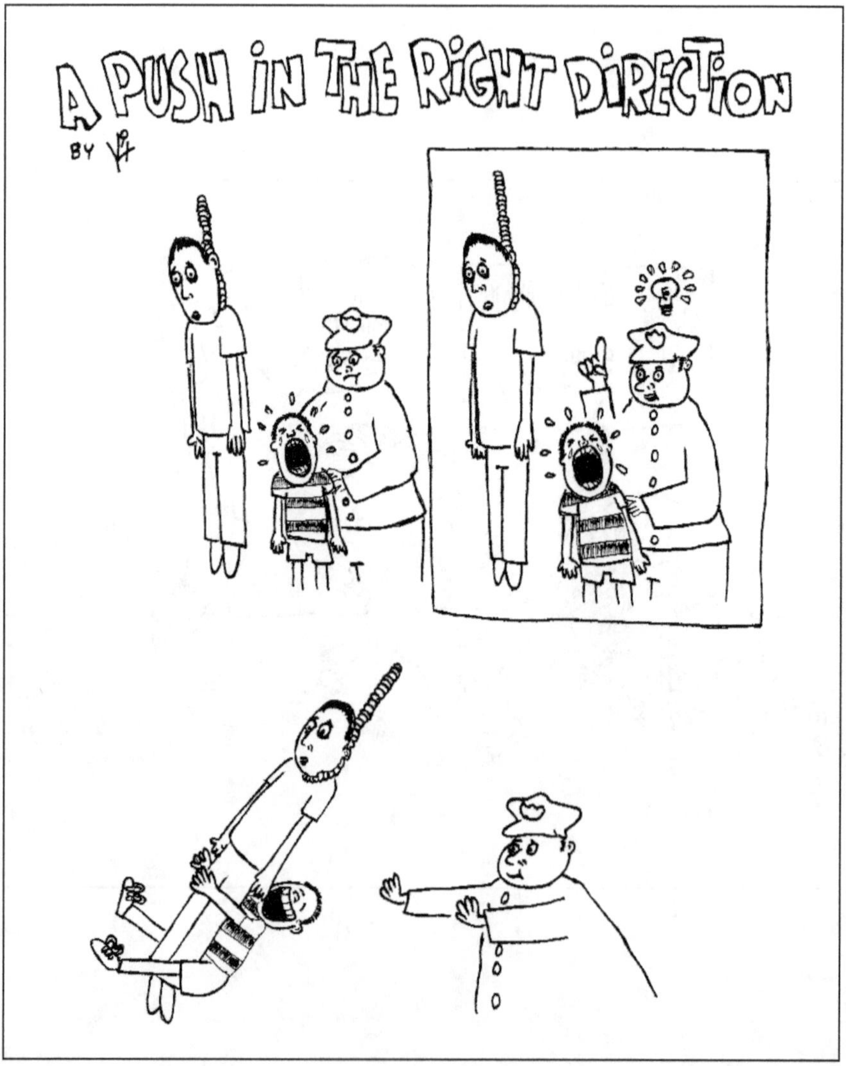
A PUSH IN THE RIGHT DIRECTION
BY

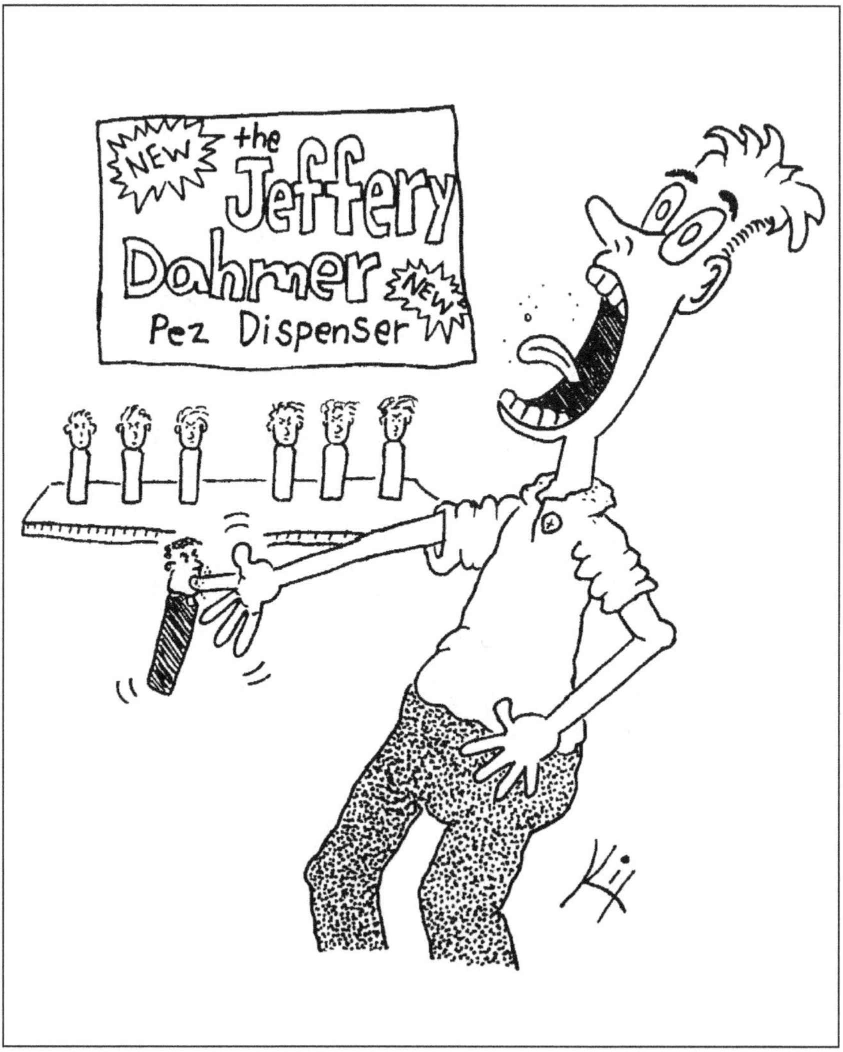
NEW
the
Jeffery
Dahmer
NEW
Pez Dispenser

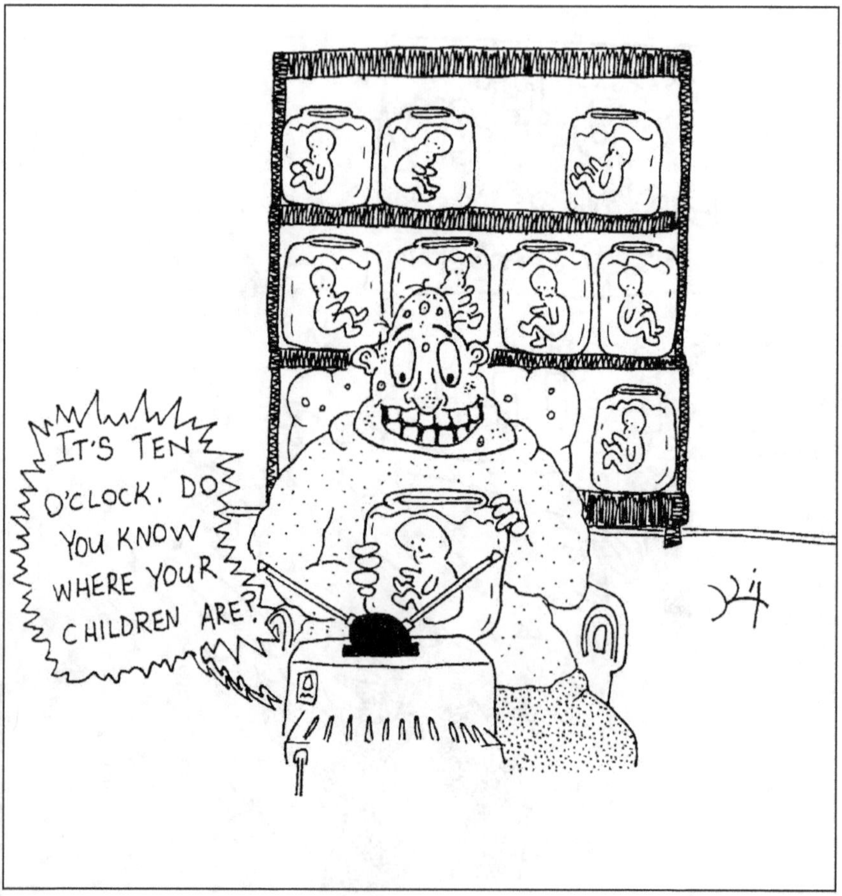
IT'S TEN O'CLOCK. DO YOU KNOW WHERE YOUR CHILDREN ARE?

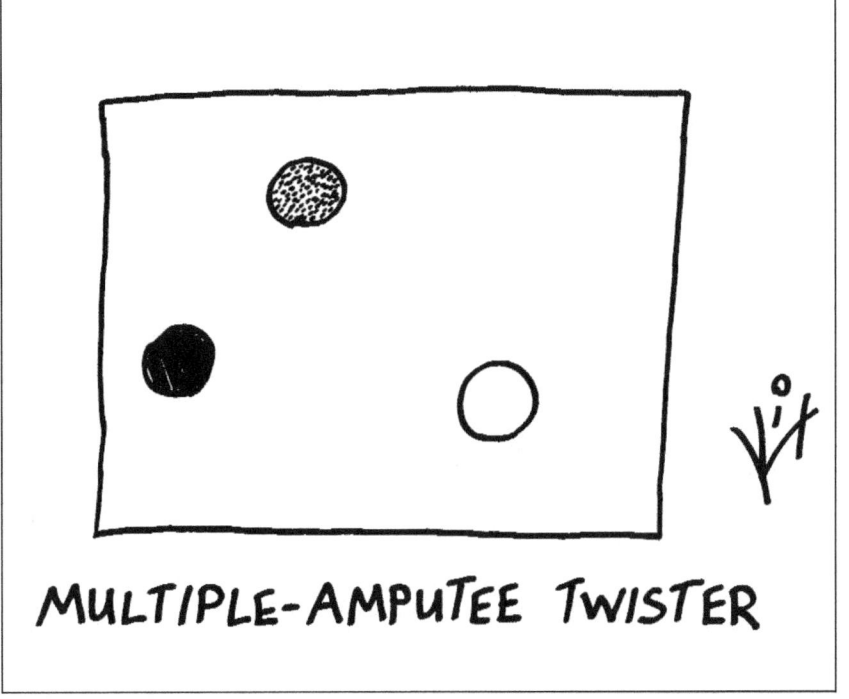

MULTIPLE-AMPUTEE TWISTER

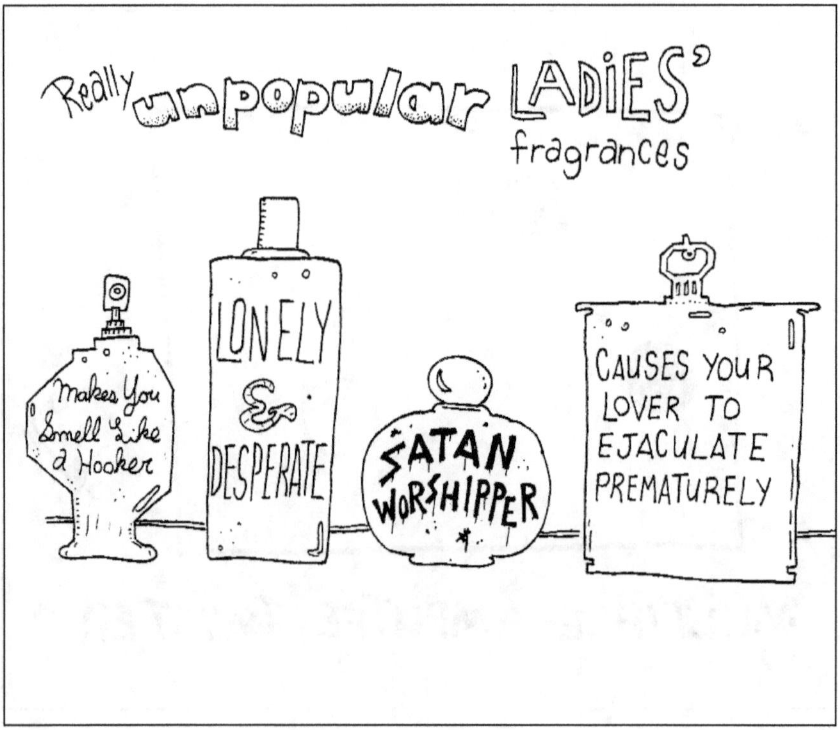
Really unpopular LADIES' fragrances
Makes You Smell Like a Hooker
LONELY & DESPERATE
SATAN WORSHIPPER
CAUSES YOUR LOVER TO EJACULATE PREMATURELY

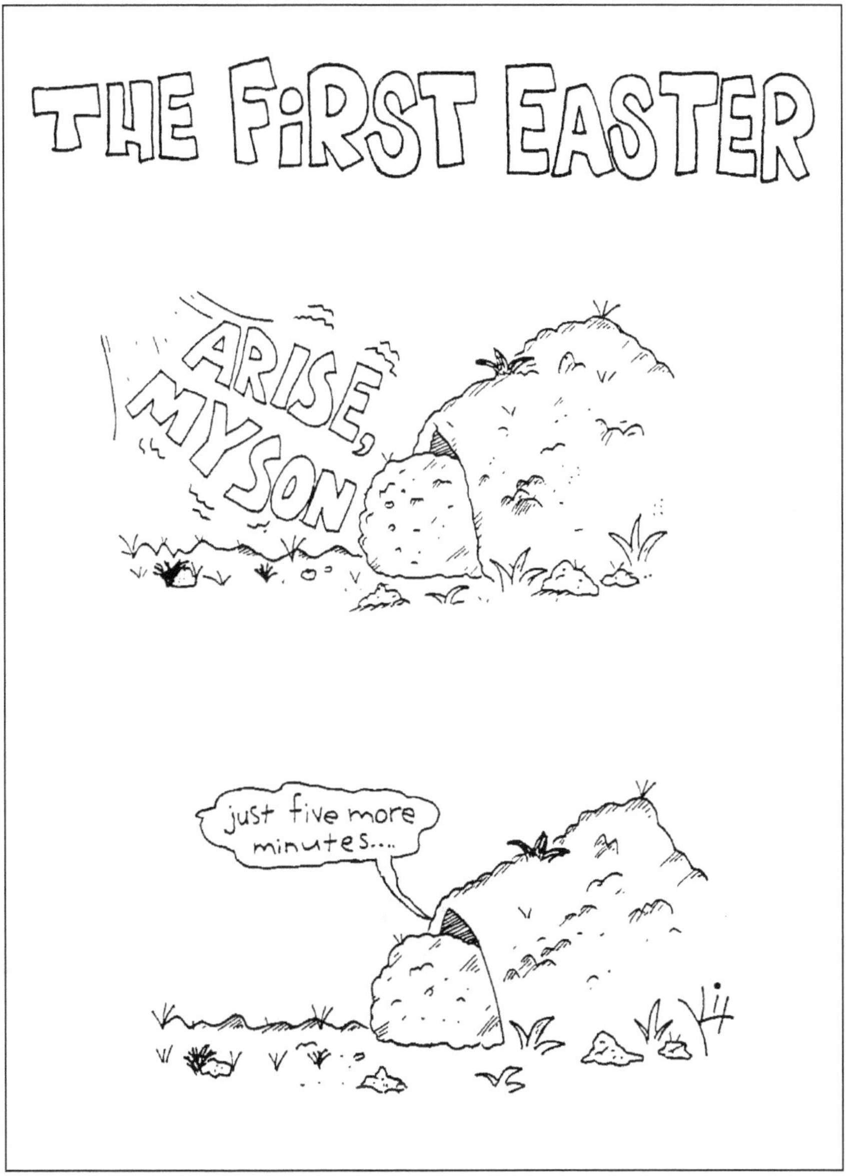
THE FIRST EASTER
ARISE, MY SON
just five more minutes....

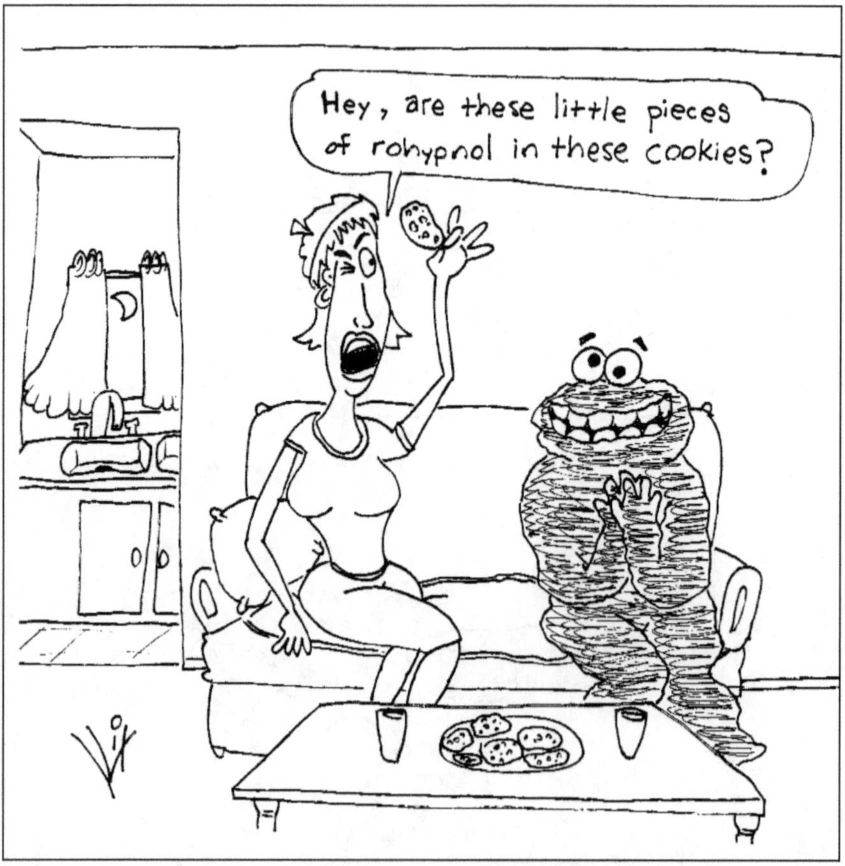
Hey, are these little pieces of rohypnol in these cookies?

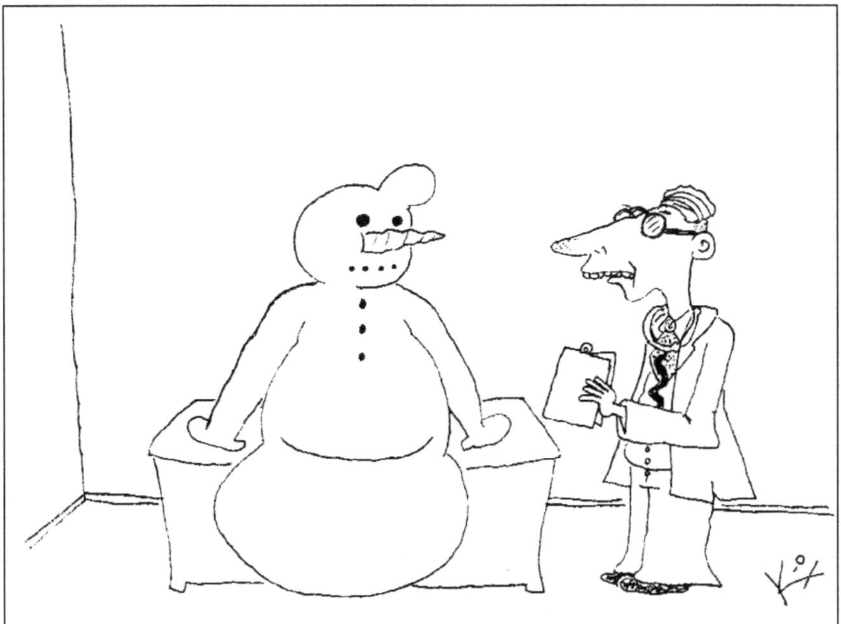

"It's not a tumor; you were apparently just hit in the head with a snowball."

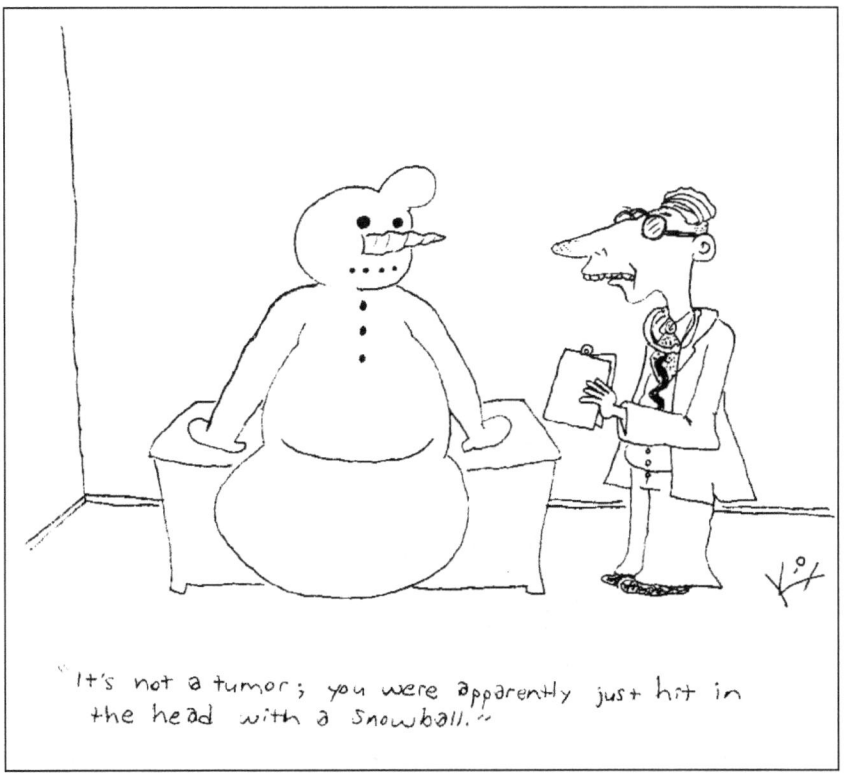

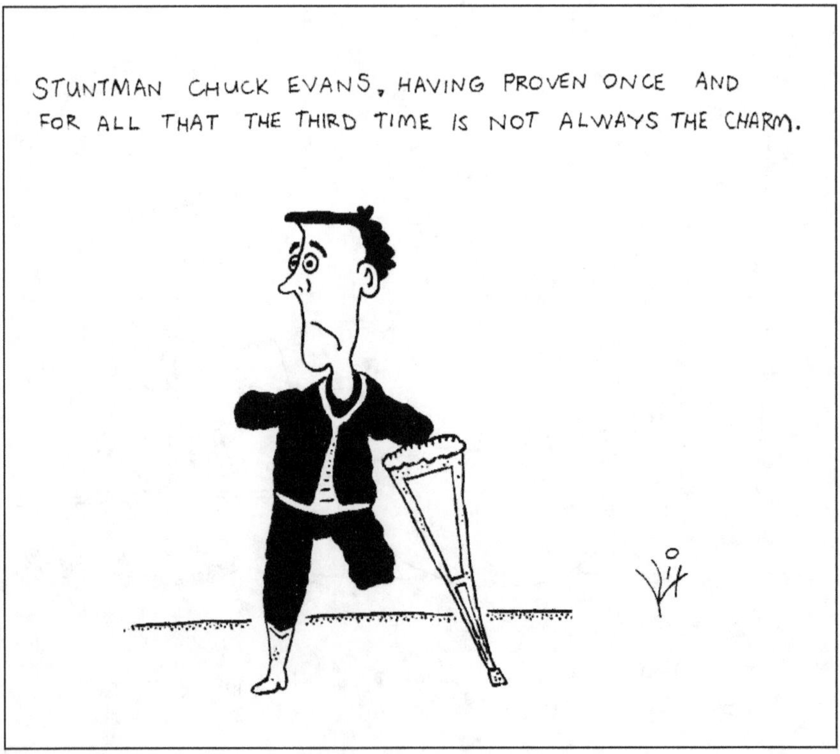

STUNTMAN CHUCK EVANS, HAVING PROVEN ONCE AND FOR ALL THAT THE THIRD TIME IS NOT ALWAYS THE CHARM.

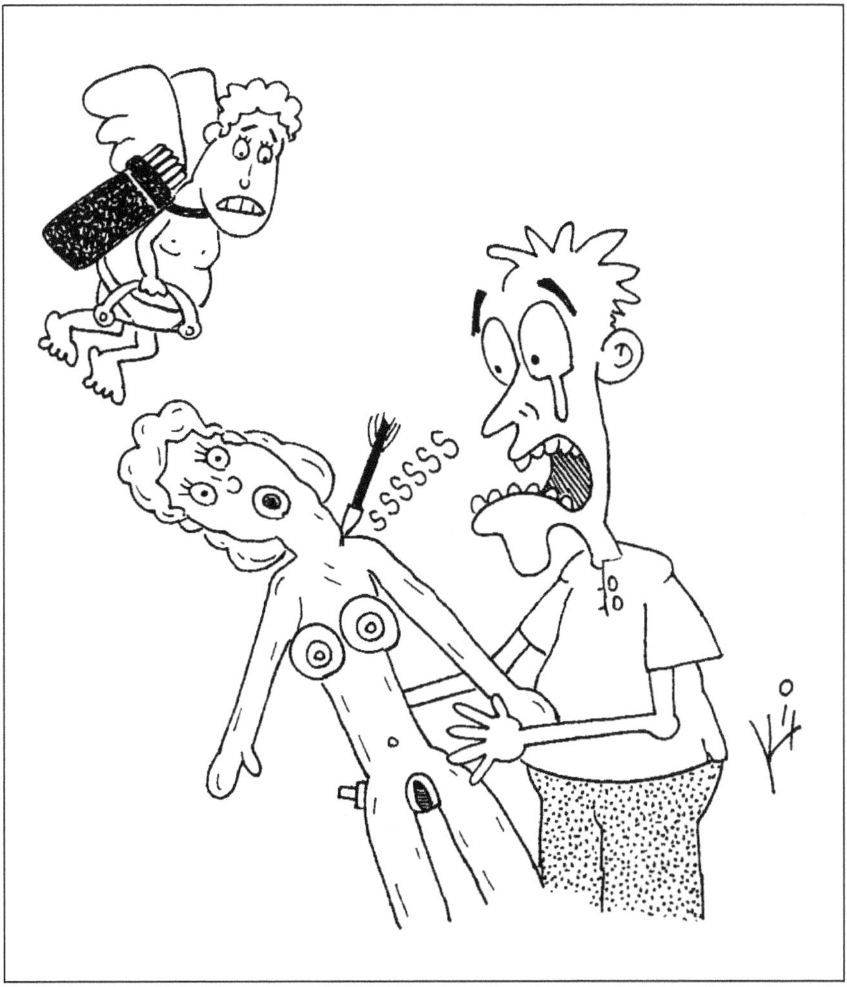
SSSSSS

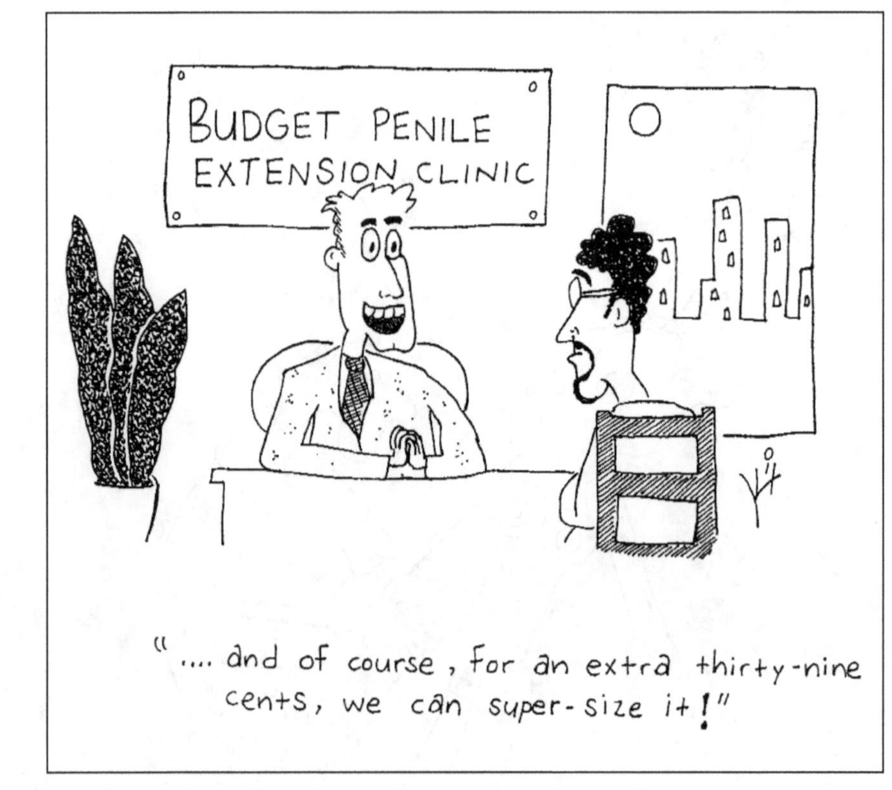
BUDGET PENILE
EXTENSION CLINIC

"…. and of course, for an extra thirty-nine cents, we can super-size it!"

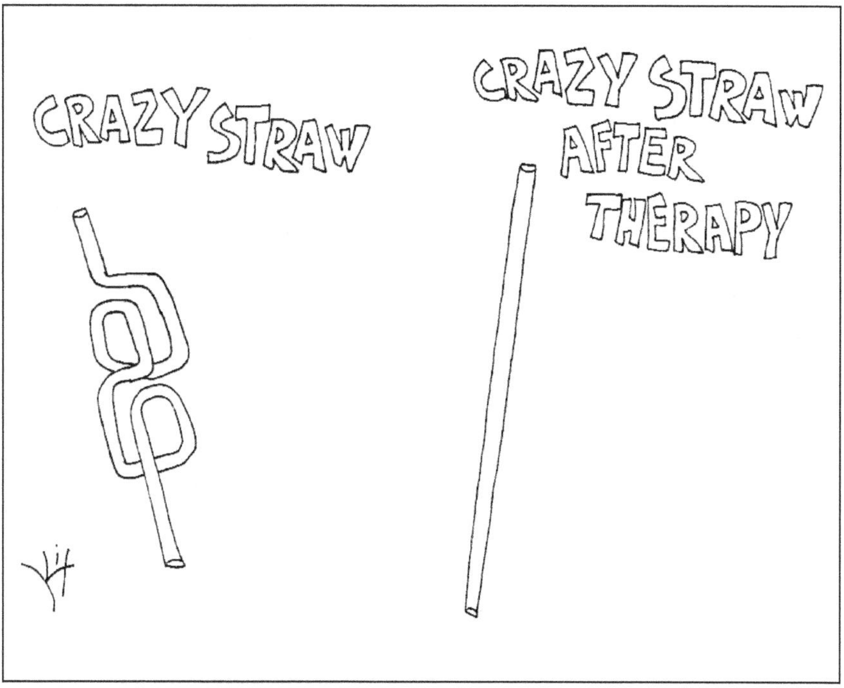
CRAZY STRAW
CRAZY STRAW AFTER THERAPY

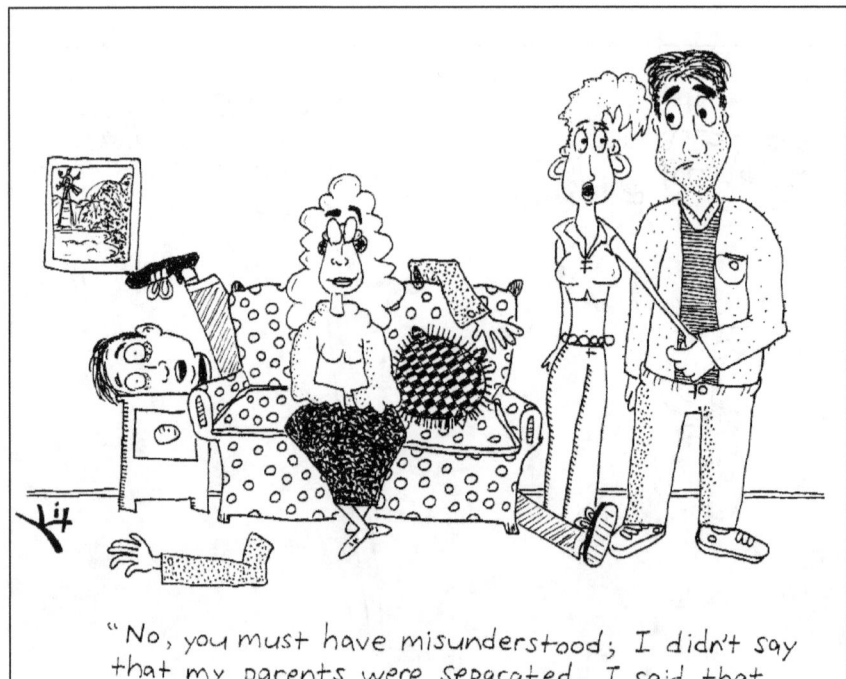

"No, you must have misunderstood; I didn't say that my parents were separated, I said that my <u>father</u> was separated."

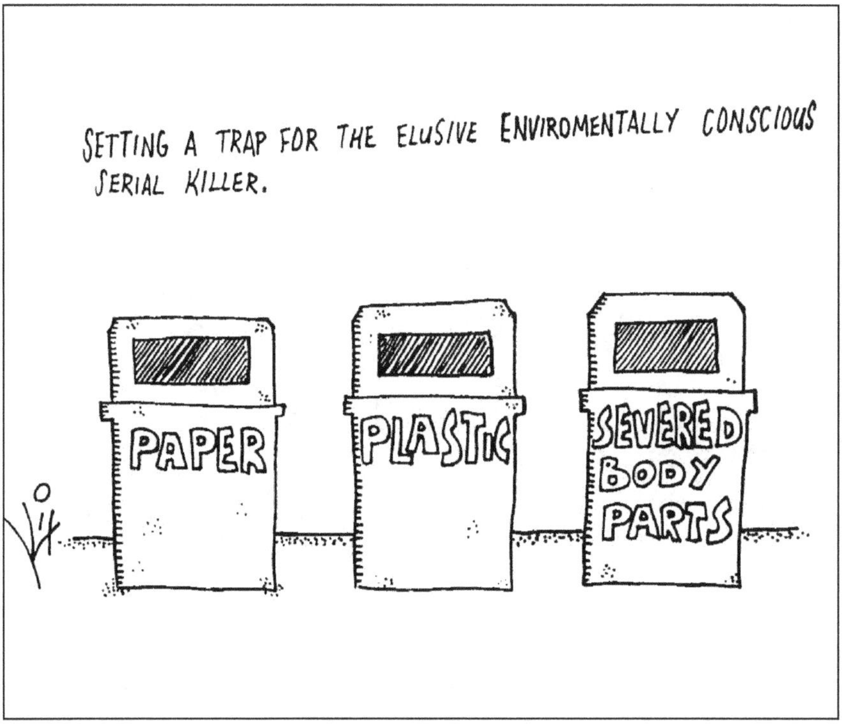
SETTING A TRAP FOR THE ELUSIVE ENVIROMENTALLY CONSCIOUS SERIAL KILLER.
PAPER
PLASTIC
SEVERED BODY PARTS

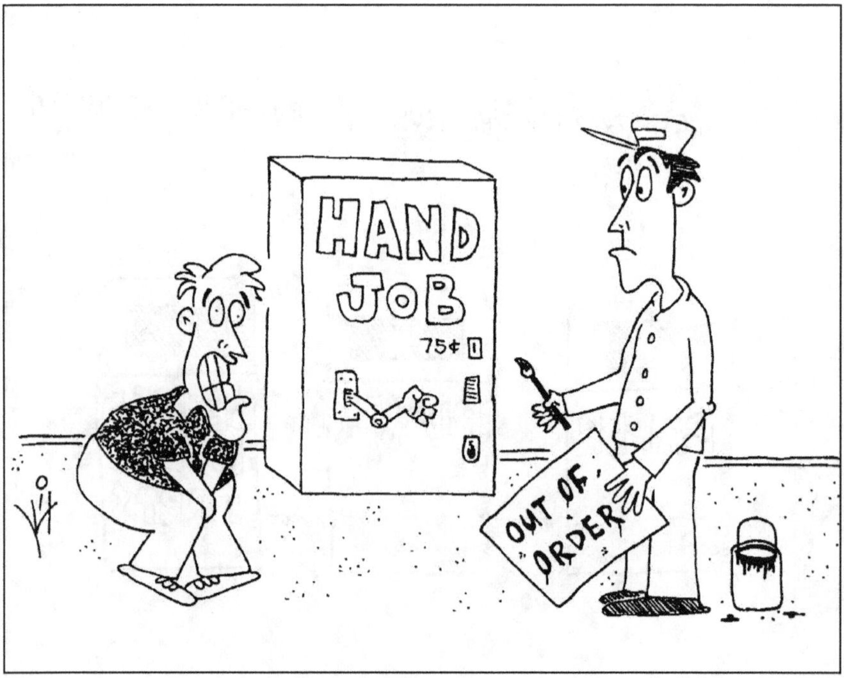
HAND
JOB
75¢
OUT OF ORDER

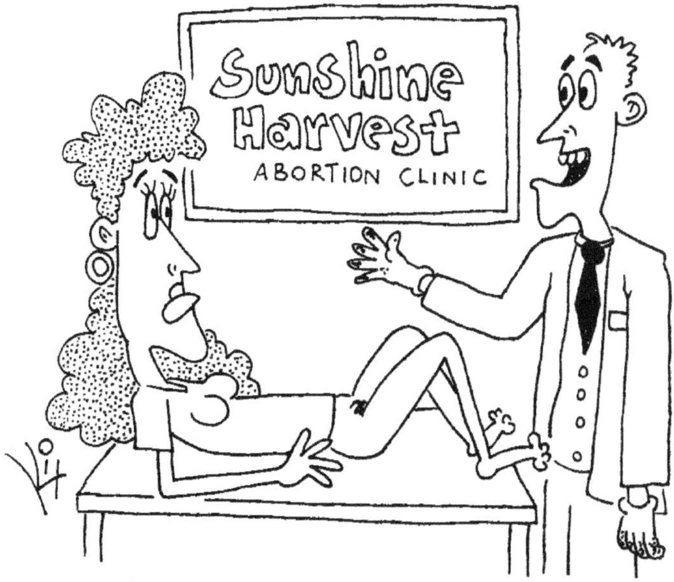
Sunshine Harvest
ABORTION CLINIC

"IT WAS TWINS, MS. LIPTON; FORTUNATELY, WE'RE HAVING A TWO FOR ONE SPECIAL THIS WEEK!"

THE JAYNE MANSFIELD PEZ DISPENSER
PEZ
PEZ

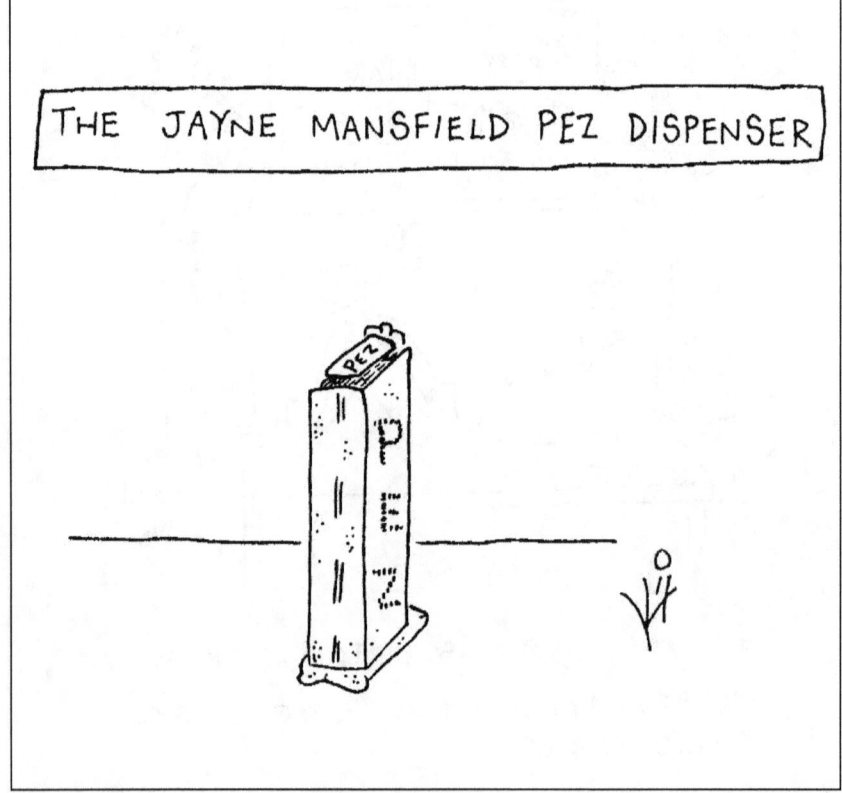

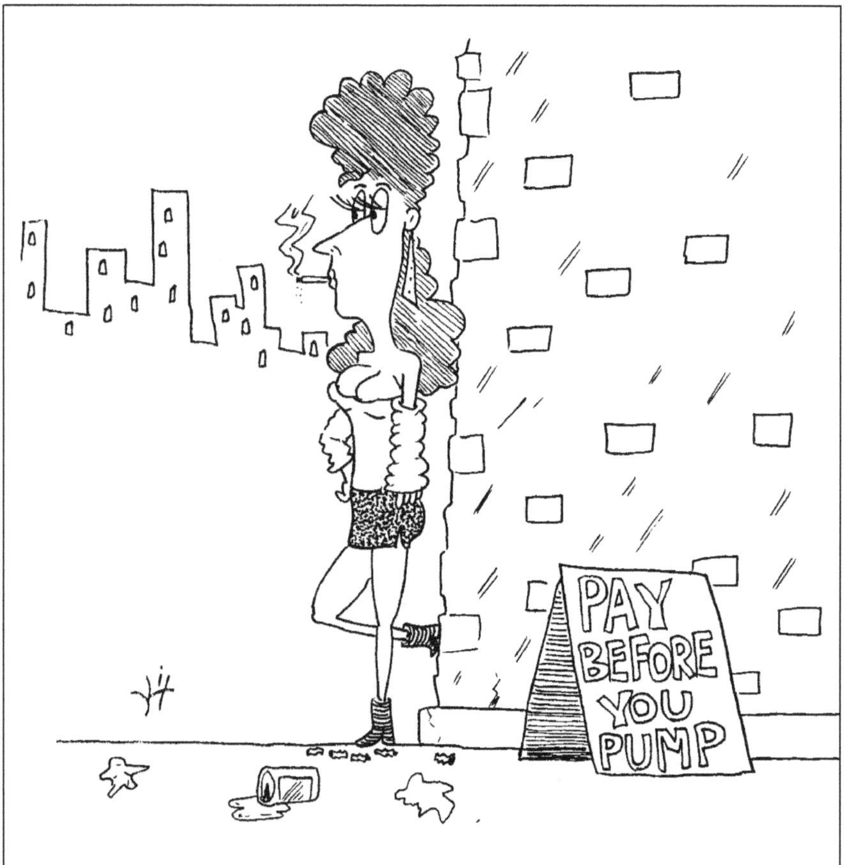
PAY
BEFORE
YOU
PUMP

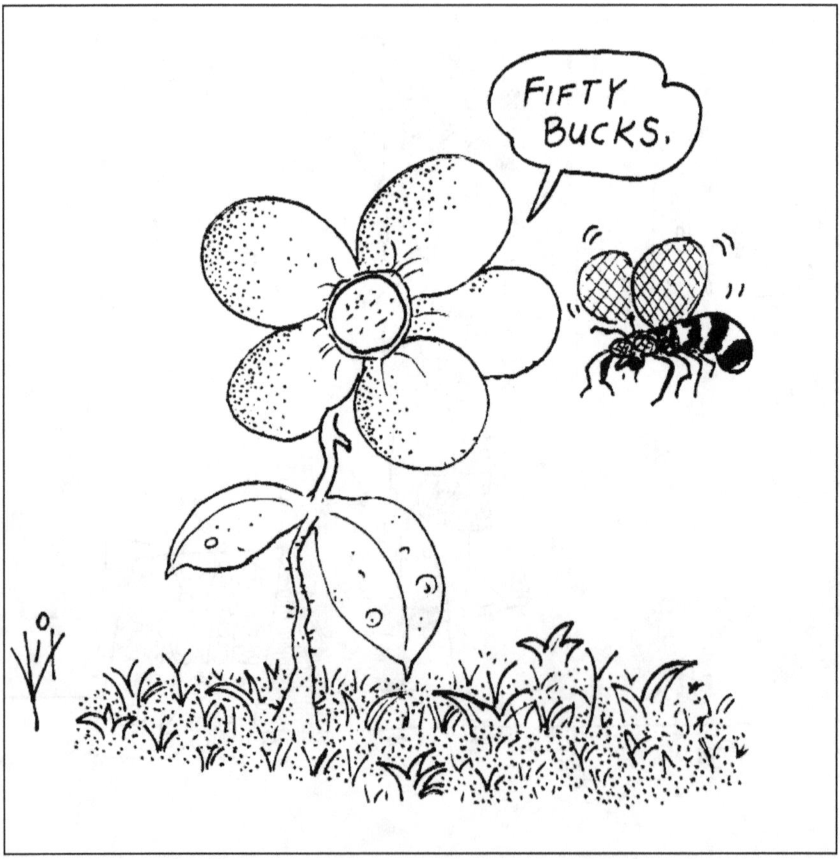
FIFTY BUCKS.

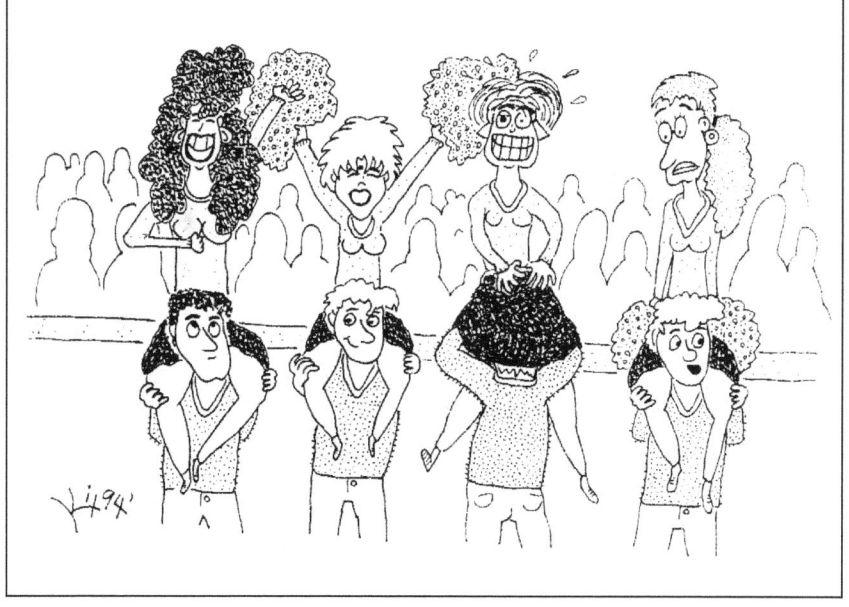

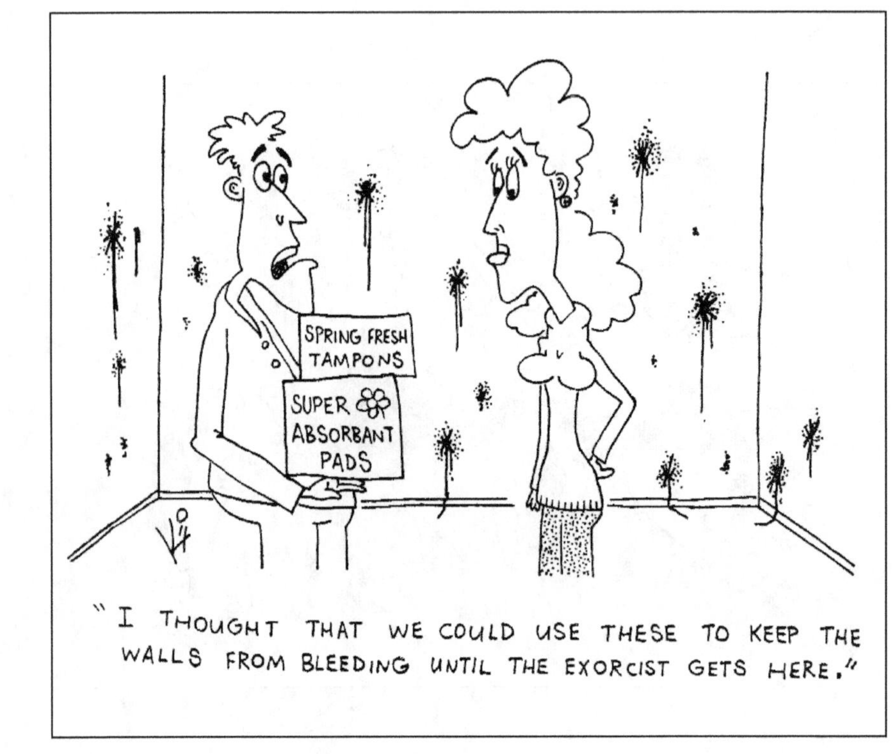
SPRING FRESH
TAMPONS
SUPER
ABSORBANT
PADS

"I THOUGHT THAT WE COULD USE THESE TO KEEP THE WALLS FROM BLEEDING UNTIL THE EXORCIST GETS HERE."

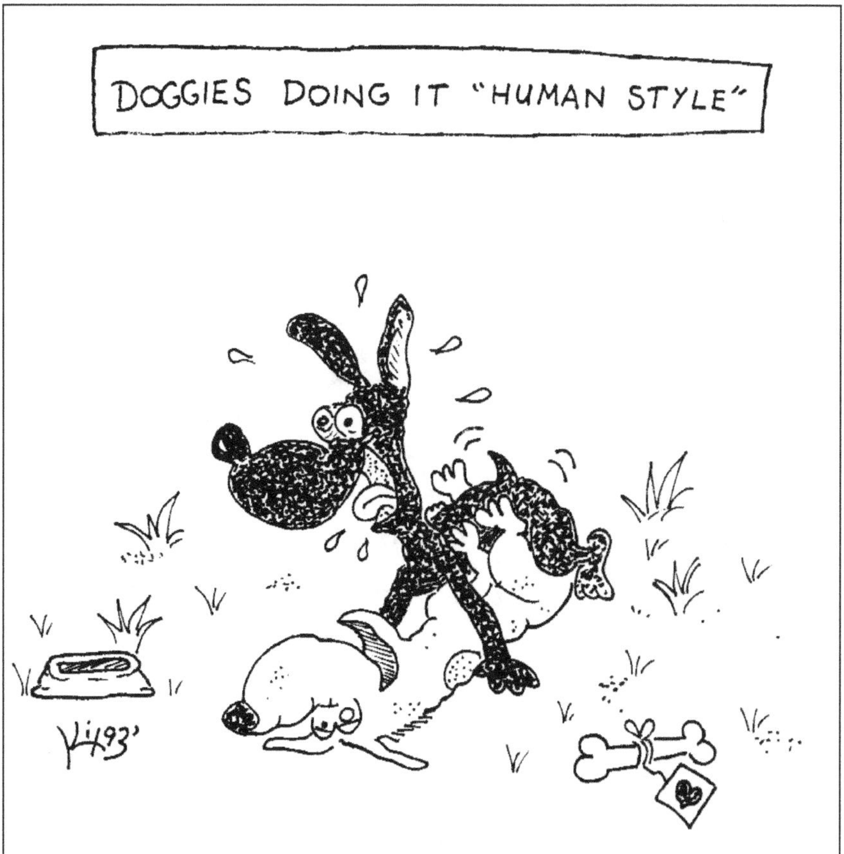
DOGGIES DOING IT "HUMAN STYLE"
Li 93'

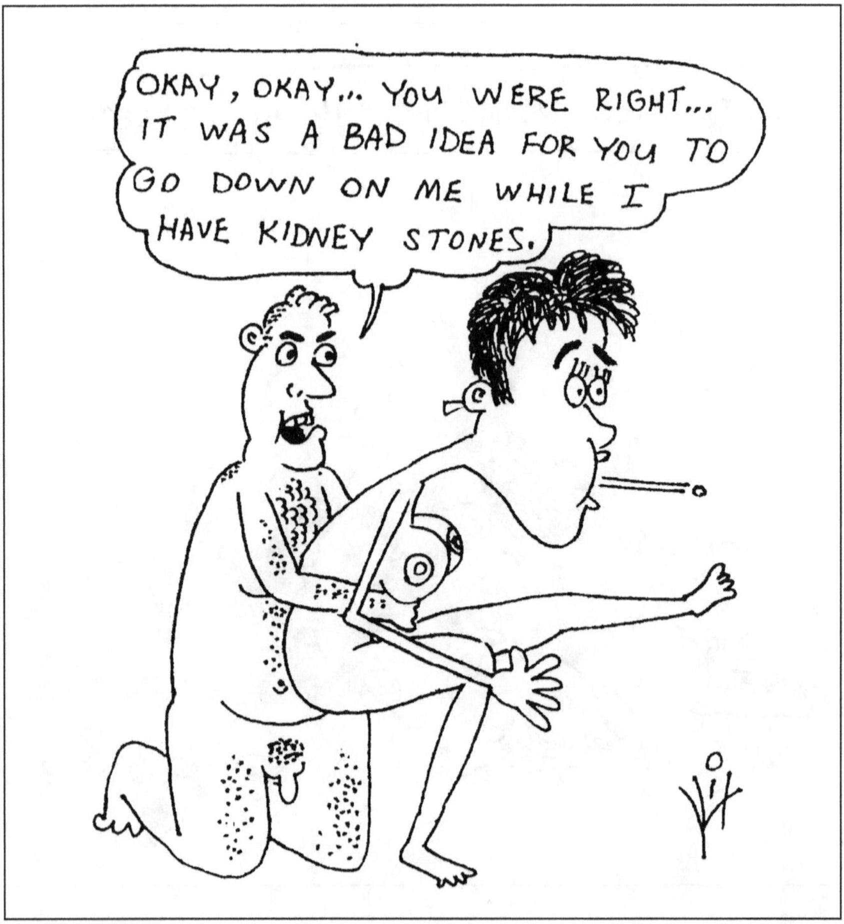
OKAY, OKAY... YOU WERE RIGHT... IT WAS A BAD IDEA FOR YOU TO GO DOWN ON ME WHILE I HAVE KIDNEY STONES.

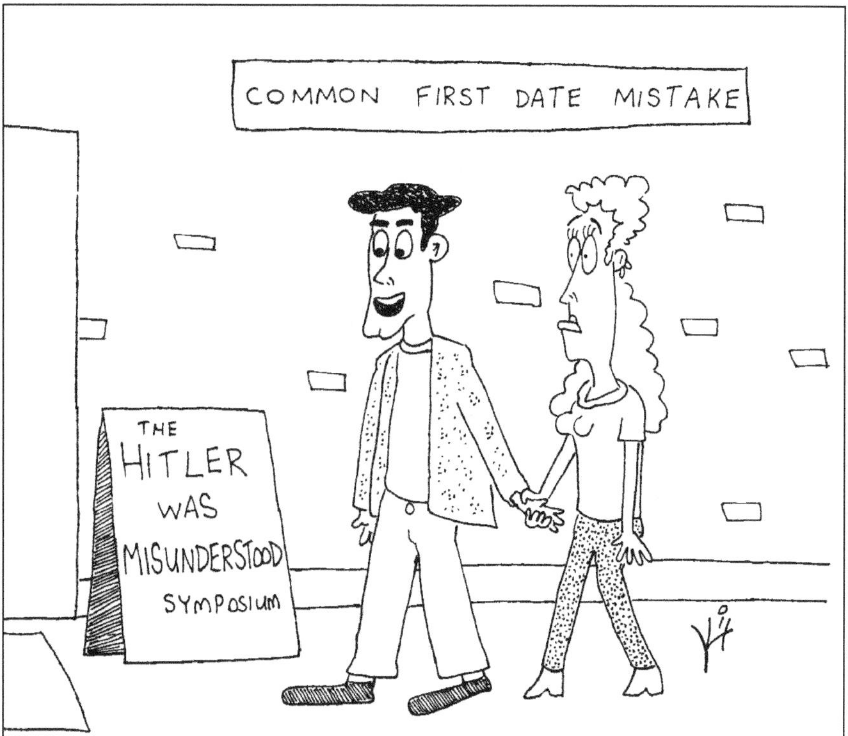
COMMON FIRST DATE MISTAKE
THE HITLER WAS MISUNDERSTOOD SYMPOSIUM

"Say, this looks interesting!"

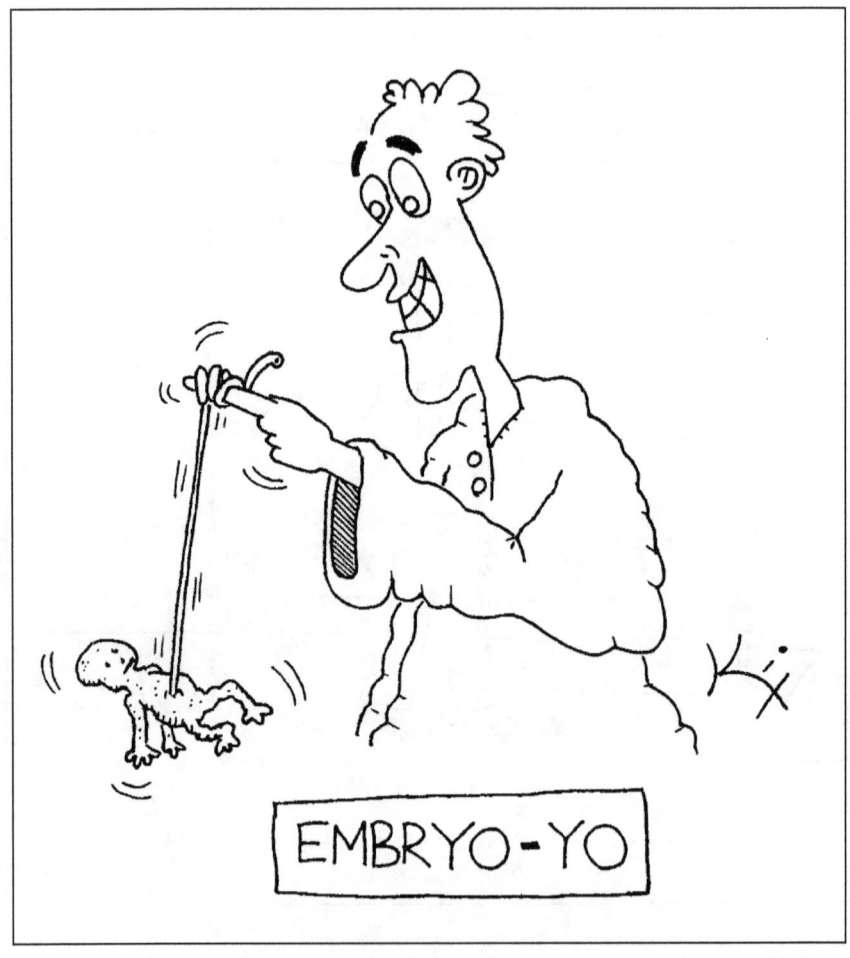

EMBRYO-YO

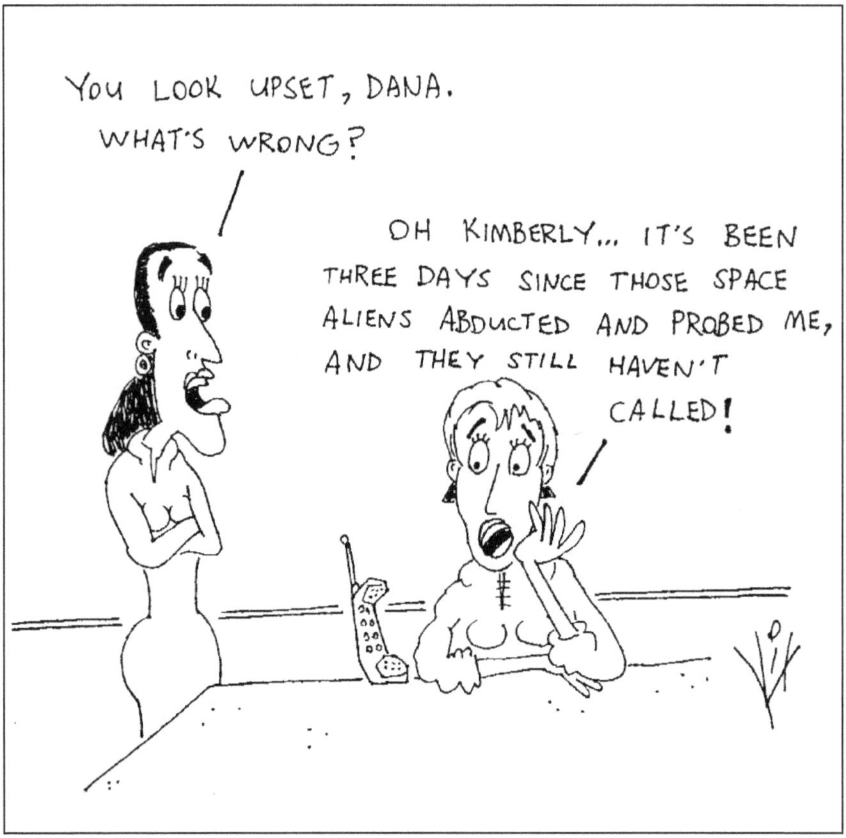
YOU LOOK UPSET, DANA. WHAT'S WRONG?
OH KIMBERLY... IT'S BEEN THREE DAYS SINCE THOSE SPACE ALIENS ABDUCTED AND PROBED ME, AND THEY STILL HAVEN'T CALLED!

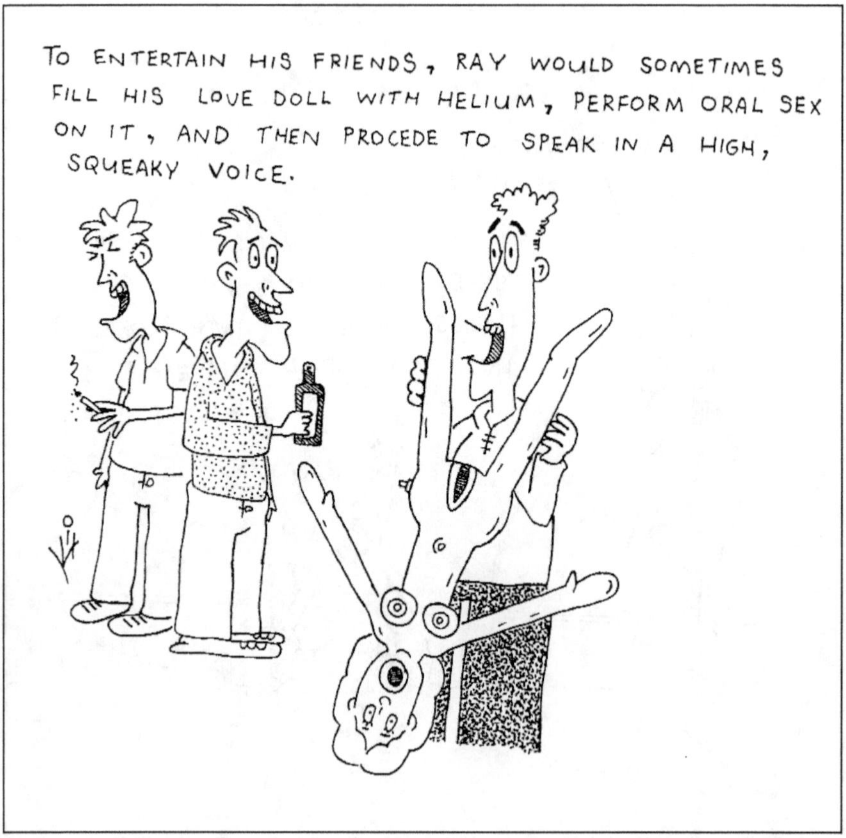
TO ENTERTAIN HIS FRIENDS, RAY WOULD SOMETIMES FILL HIS LOVE DOLL WITH HELIUM, PERFORM ORAL SEX ON IT, AND THEN PROCEDE TO SPEAK IN A HIGH, SQUEAKY VOICE.

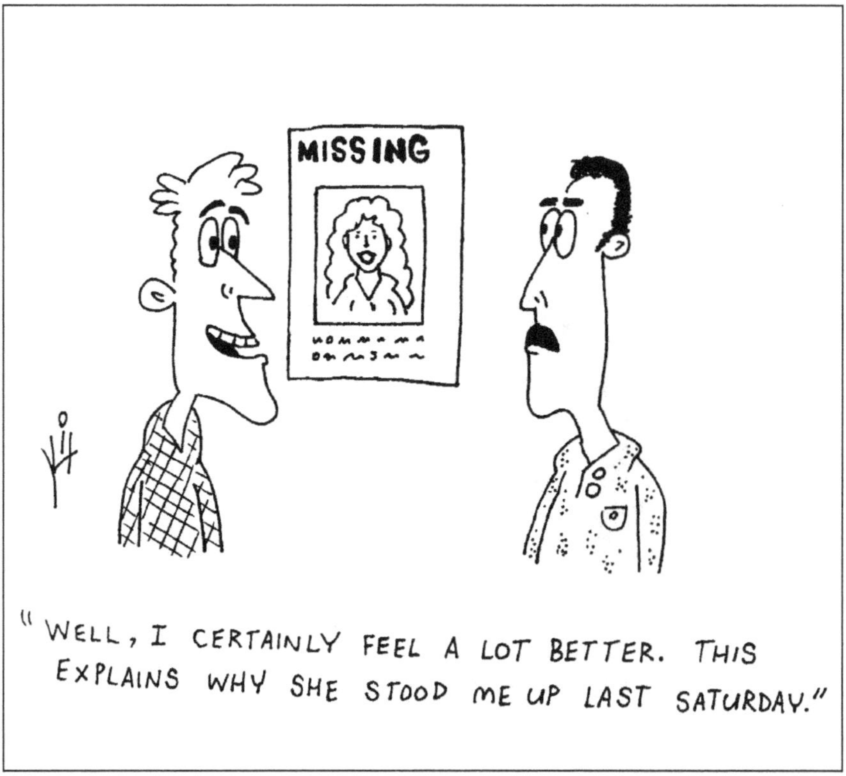
MISSING

"Well, I certainly feel a lot better. This explains why she stood me up last Saturday."

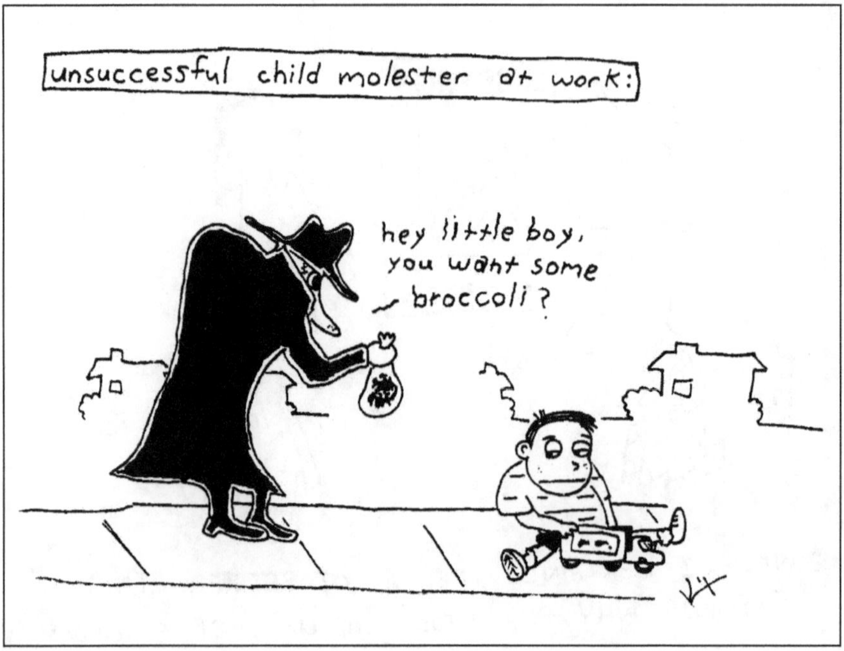
unsuccessful child molester at work:
hey little boy, you want some broccoli?

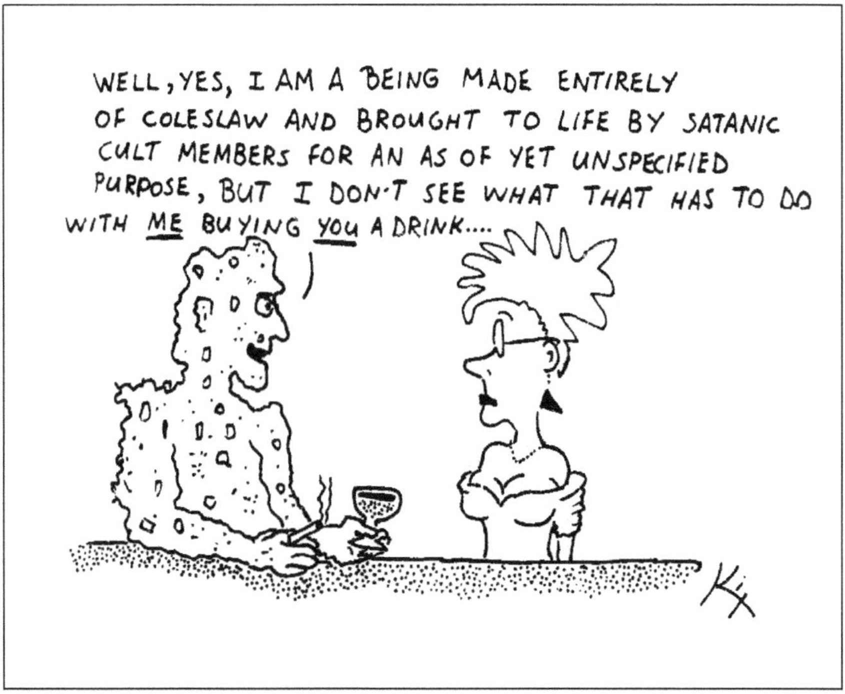
WELL, YES, I AM A BEING MADE ENTIRELY OF COLESLAW AND BROUGHT TO LIFE BY SATANIC CULT MEMBERS FOR AN AS OF YET UNSPECIFIED PURPOSE, BUT I DON'T SEE WHAT THAT HAS TO DO WITH ME BUYING YOU A DRINK....

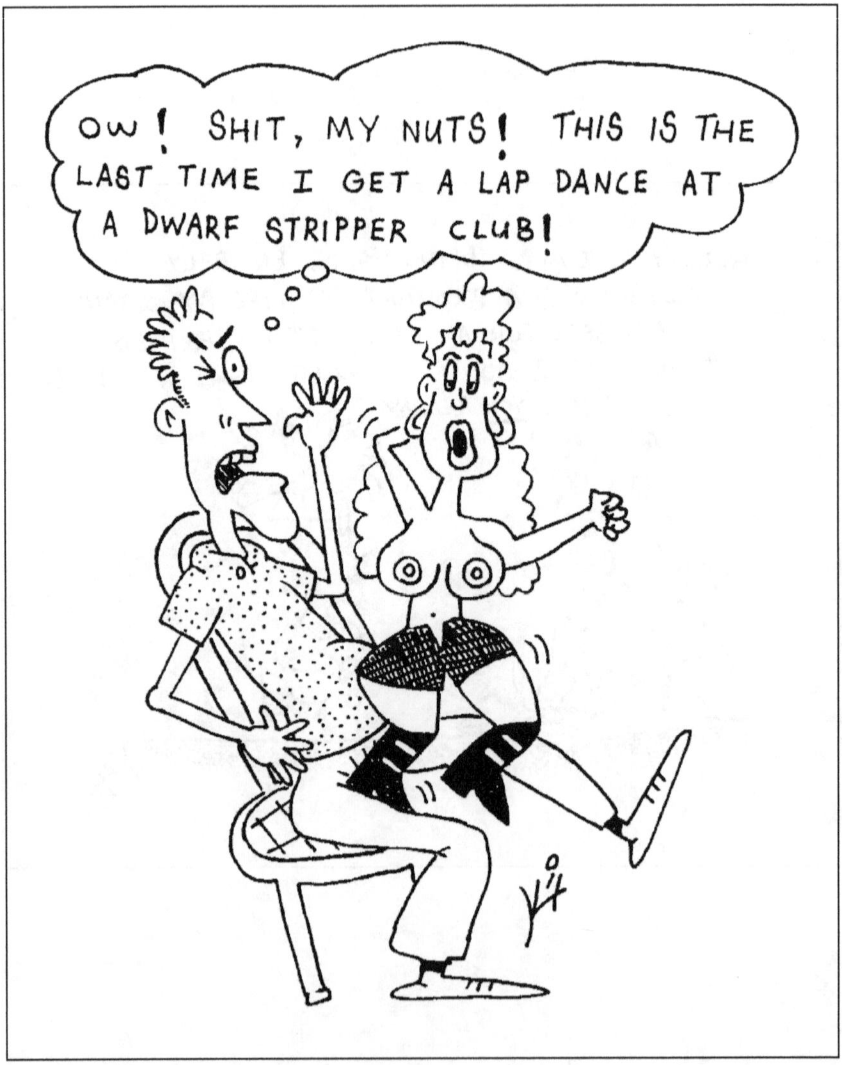
OW! SHIT, MY NUTS! THIS IS THE LAST TIME I GET A LAP DANCE AT A DWARF STRIPPER CLUB!

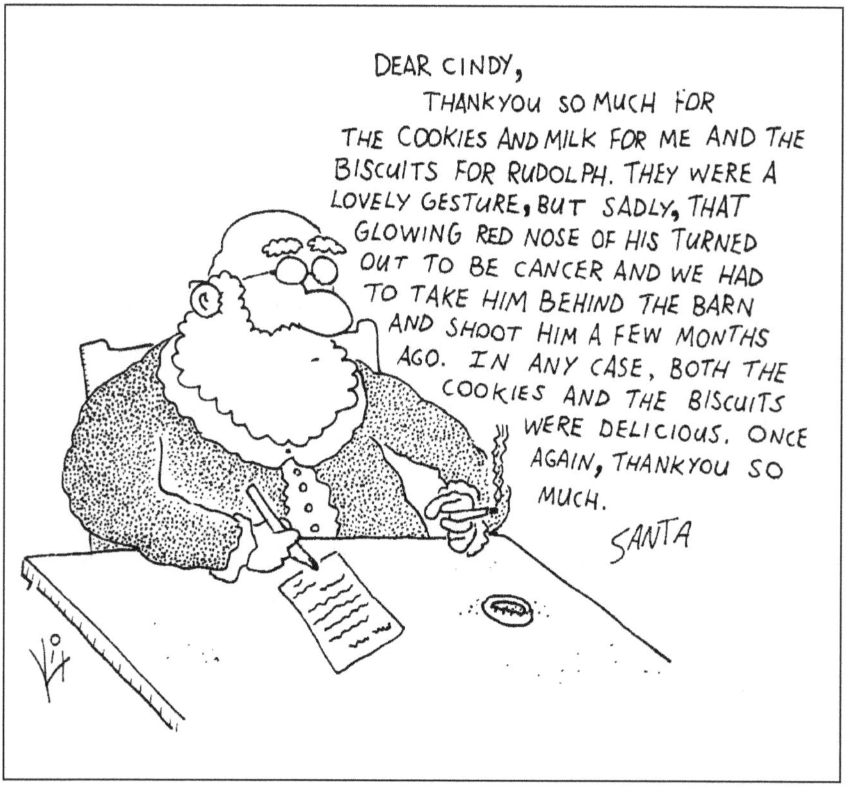
DEAR CINDY,
THANKYOU SO MUCH FOR THE COOKIES AND MILK FOR ME AND THE BISCUITS FOR RUDOLPH. THEY WERE A LOVELY GESTURE, BUT SADLY, THAT GLOWING RED NOSE OF HIS TURNED OUT TO BE CANCER AND WE HAD TO TAKE HIM BEHIND THE BARN AND SHOOT HIM A FEW MONTHS AGO. IN ANY CASE, BOTH THE COOKIES AND THE BISCUITS WERE DELICIOUS. ONCE AGAIN, THANKYOU SO MUCH.
SANTA

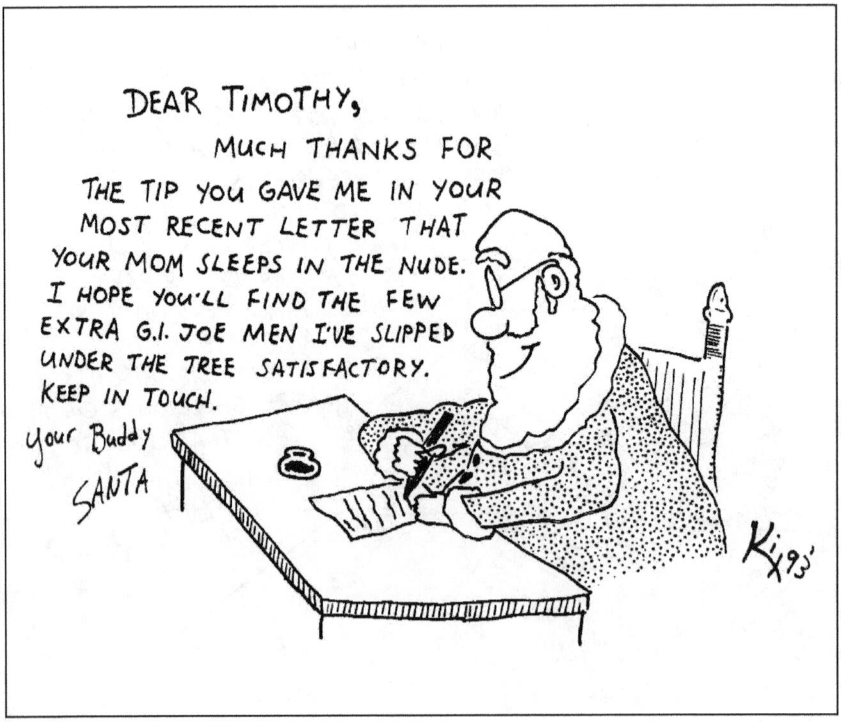
DEAR TIMOTHY,
MUCH THANKS FOR THE TIP YOU GAVE ME IN YOUR MOST RECENT LETTER THAT YOUR MOM SLEEPS IN THE NUDE. I HOPE YOU'LL FIND THE FEW EXTRA G.I. JOE MEN I'VE SLIPPED UNDER THE TREE SATISFACTORY. KEEP IN TOUCH.
Your Buddy
SANTA
Kix 93'

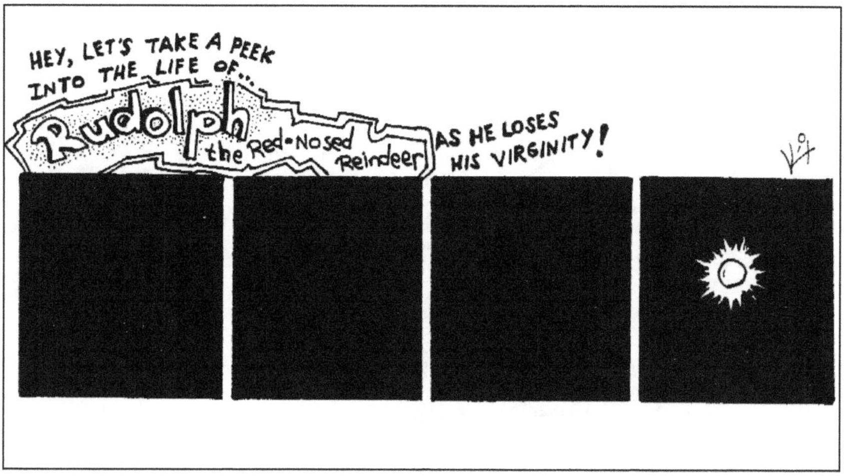
HEY, LET'S TAKE A PEEK INTO THE LIFE OF...
Rudolph the Red-Nosed Reindeer
AS HE LOSES HIS VIRGINITY!

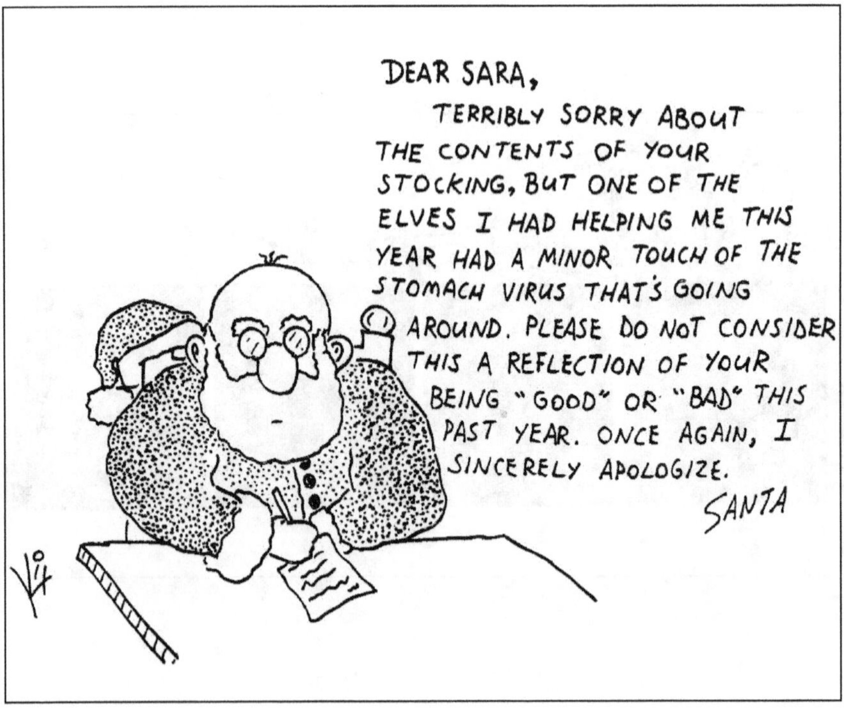
DEAR SARA,
TERRIBLY SORRY ABOUT THE CONTENTS OF YOUR STOCKING, BUT ONE OF THE ELVES I HAD HELPING ME THIS YEAR HAD A MINOR TOUCH OF THE STOMACH VIRUS THAT'S GOING AROUND. PLEASE DO NOT CONSIDER THIS A REFLECTION OF YOUR BEING "GOOD" OR "BAD" THIS PAST YEAR. ONCE AGAIN, I SINCERELY APOLOGIZE.
SANTA

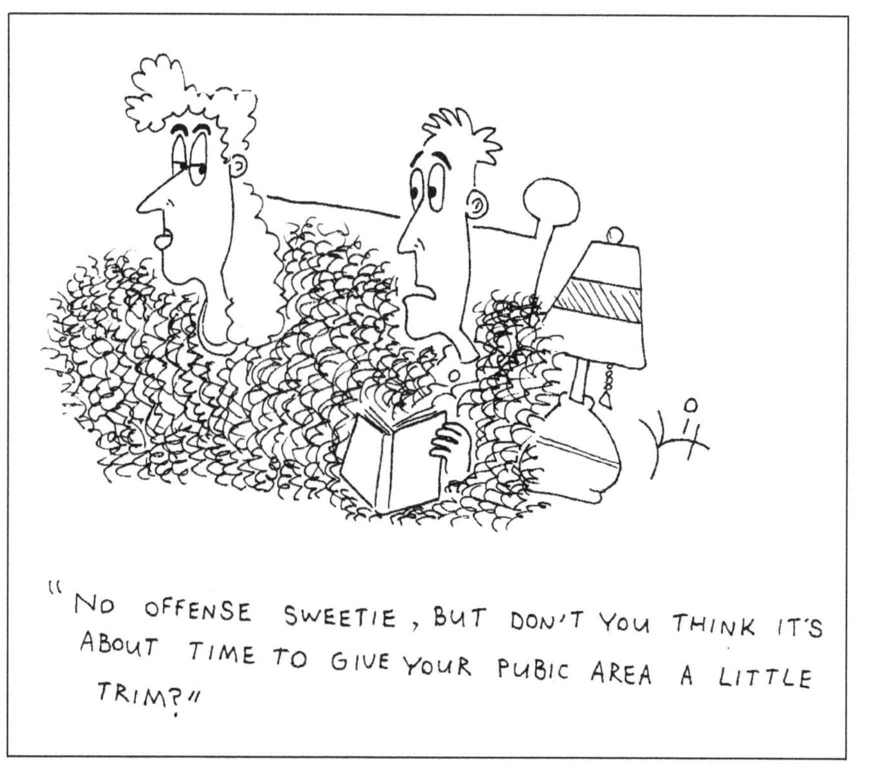

"NO OFFENSE SWEETIE, BUT DON'T YOU THINK IT'S ABOUT TIME TO GIVE YOUR PUBIC AREA A LITTLE TRIM?"

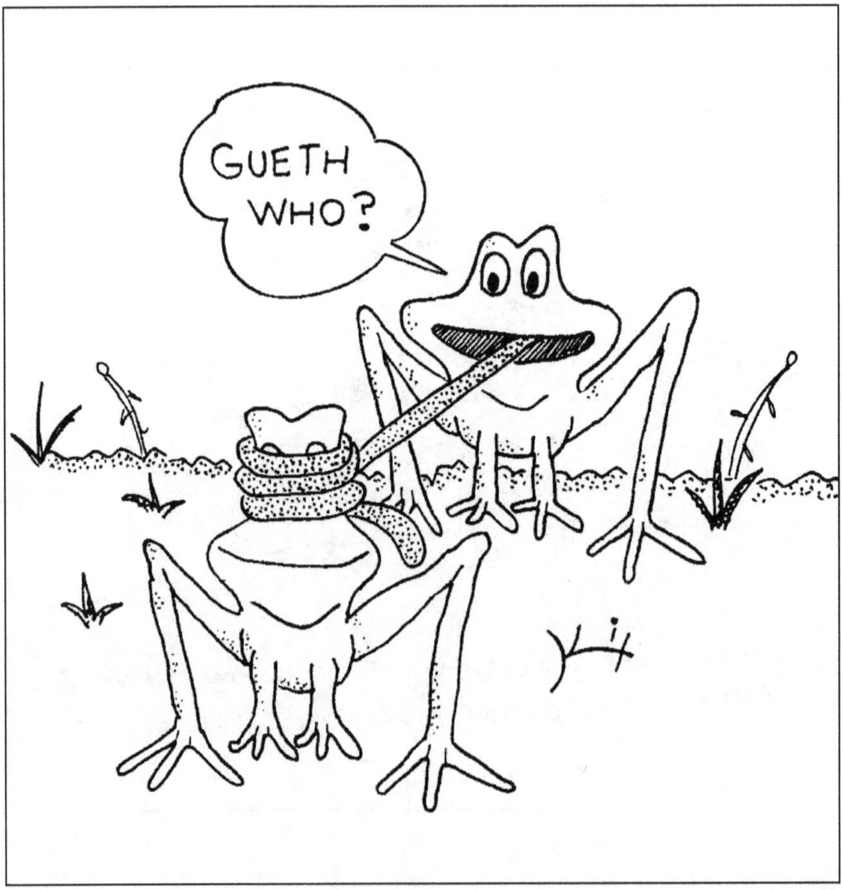
GUETH WHO?

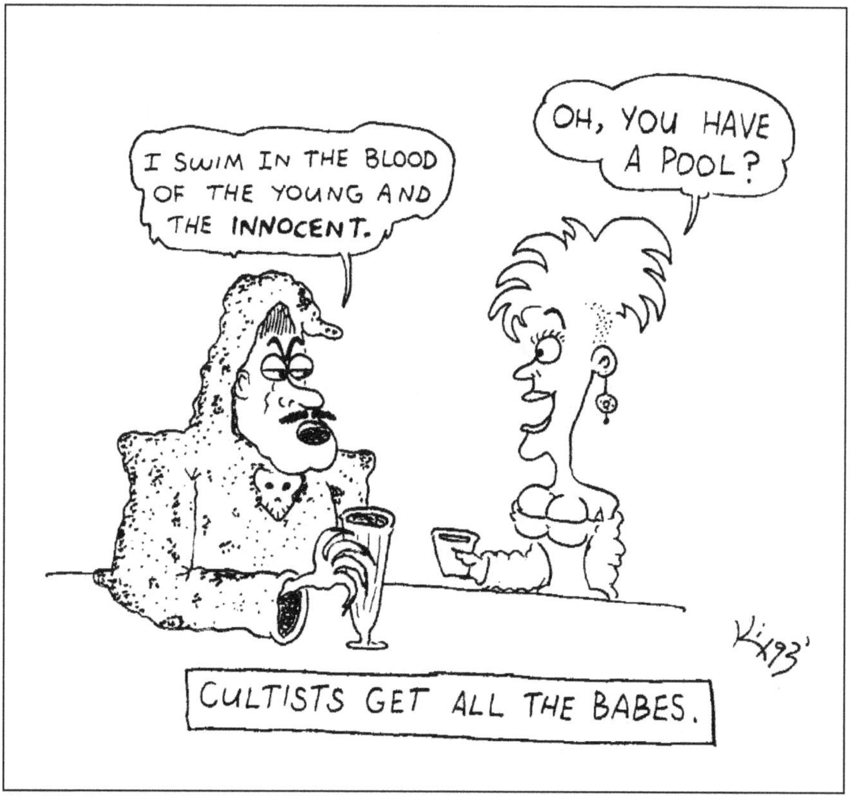
I SWIM IN THE BLOOD OF THE YOUNG AND THE INNOCENT.
OH, YOU HAVE A POOL?
CULTISTS GET ALL THE BABES.

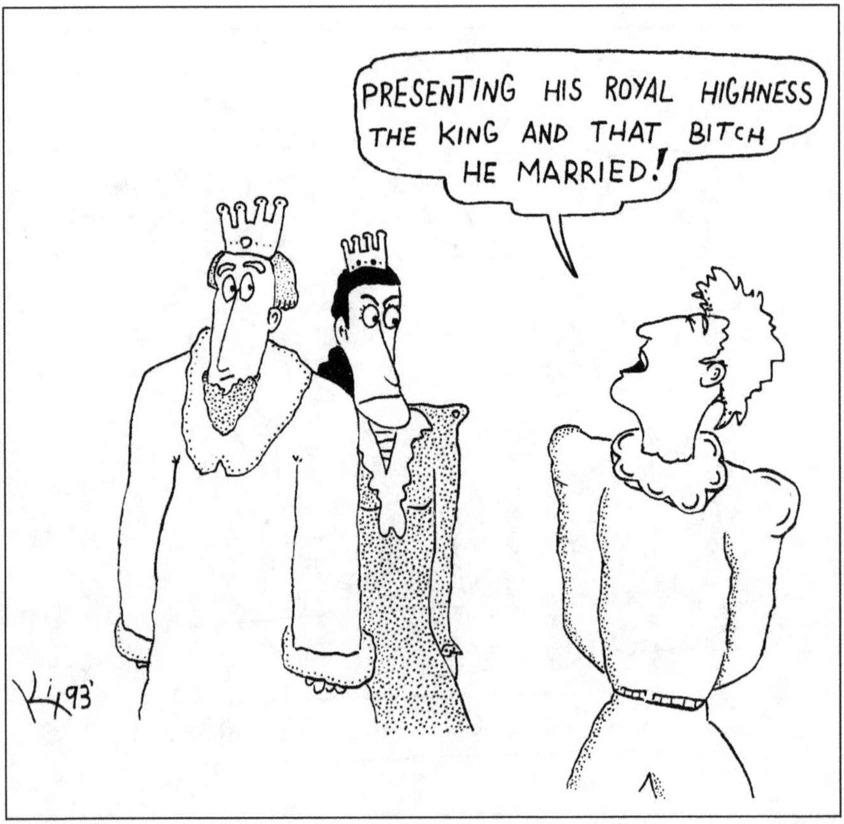
PRESENTING HIS ROYAL HIGHNESS THE KING AND THAT BITCH HE MARRIED!

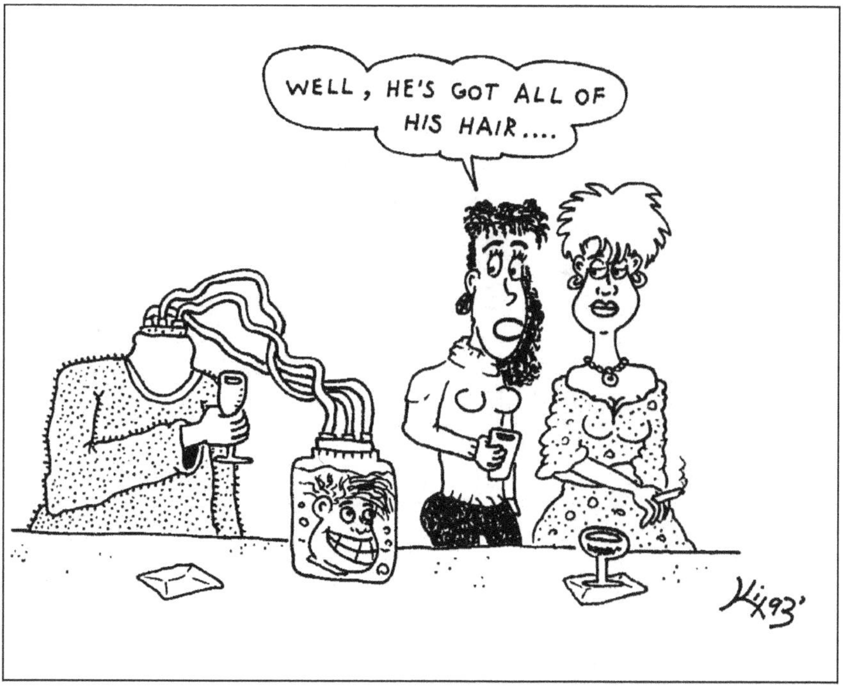
WELL, HE'S GOT ALL OF HIS HAIR....
Kix 93'

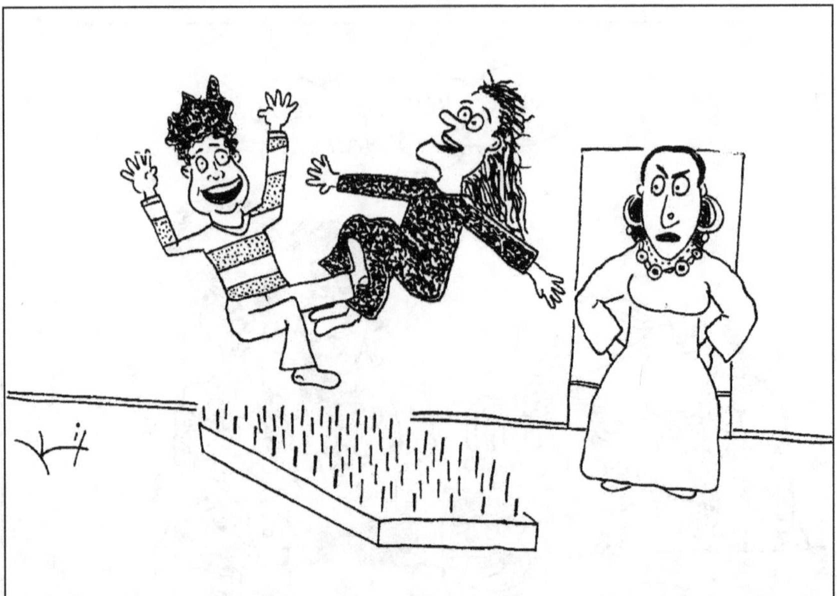

"All right you two! What have I told you about jumping on the bed?!"

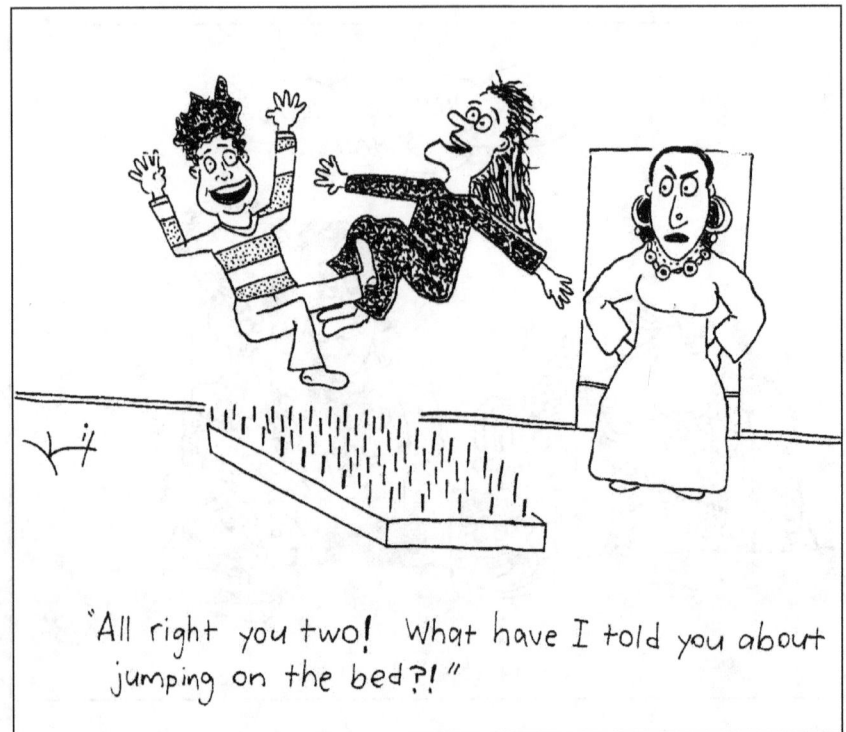

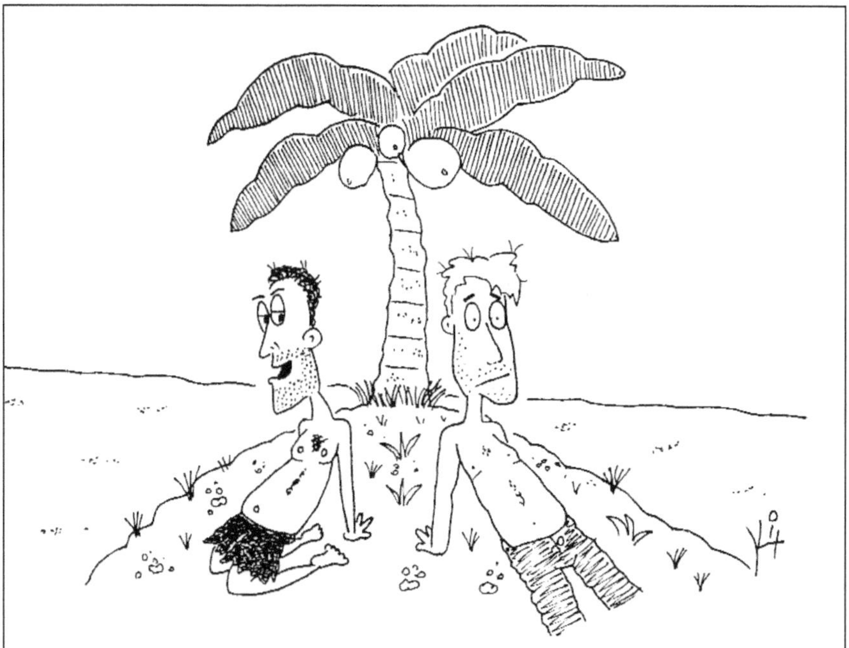

"WELL, YOU KNOW WHAT THEY SAY; IF YOU CAN'T BE WITH THE ONE YOU LOVE, LOVE THE ONE YOU'RE WITH."

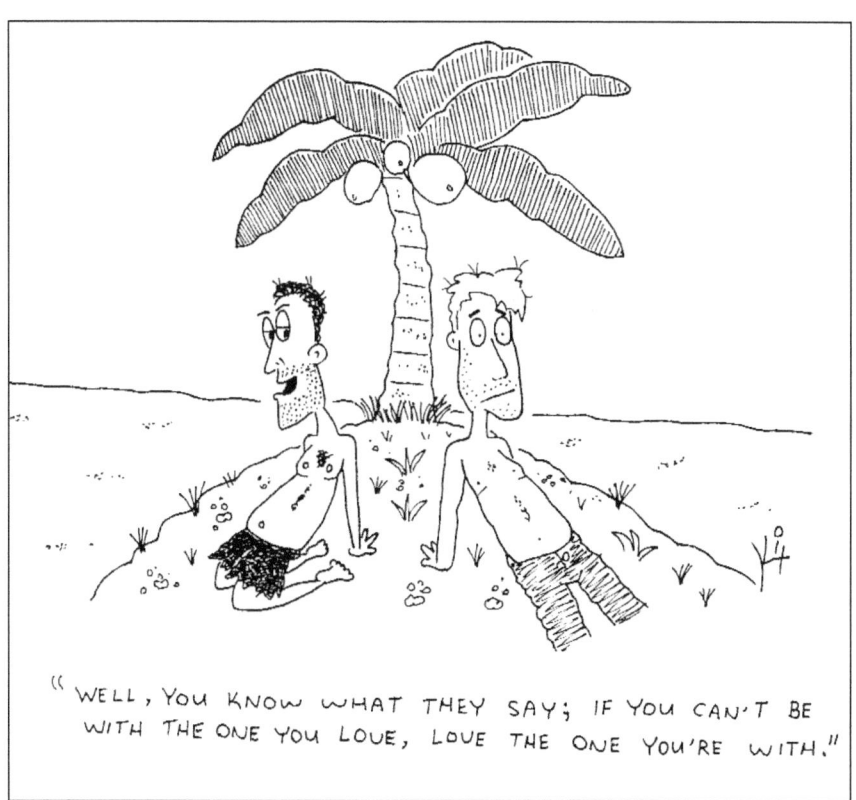

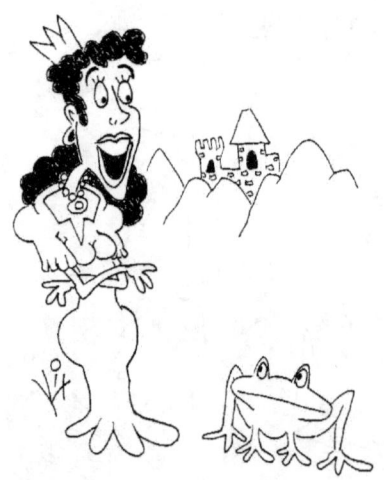

"WELL, OKAY, LET ME ASK YOU THIS: IF I KISS YOU, AND YOU TURN INTO A PRINCE, WILL YOUR TONGUE STAY AS LONG AS IT IS NOW?"

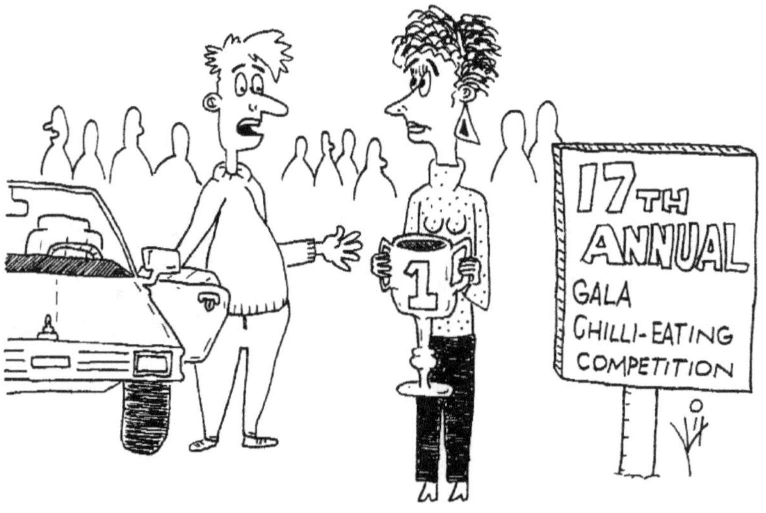
17TH
ANNUAL
GALA
CHILLI-EATING
COMPETITION
1

"No offense Arlene, but could you get a ride home from someone else? I just had my car seats reupholstered."

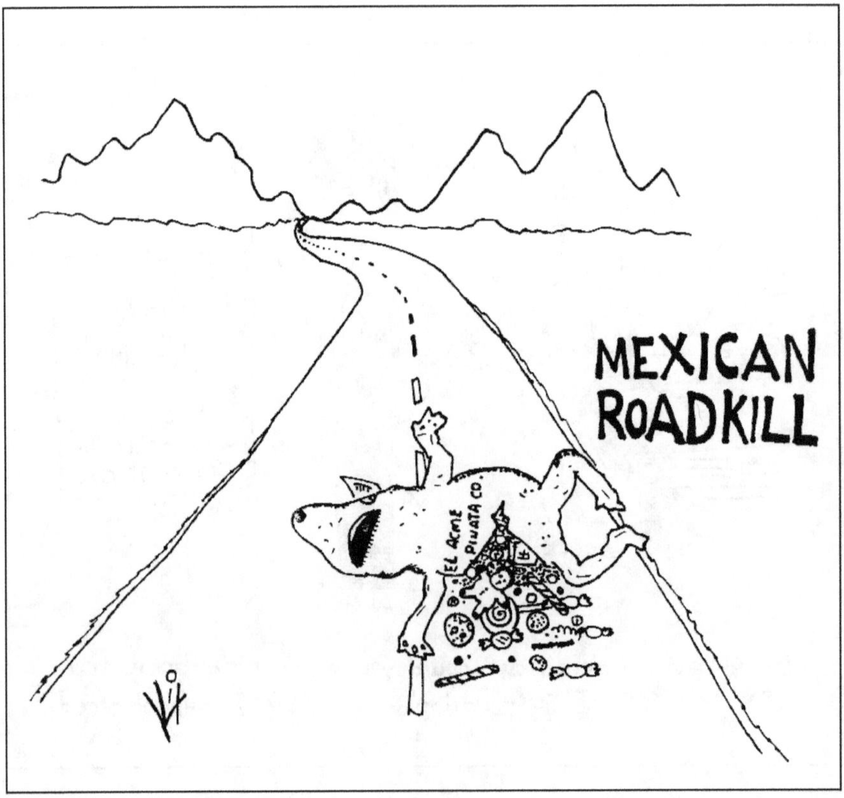
MEXICAN
ROADKILL
EL ACME
PINATA CO.

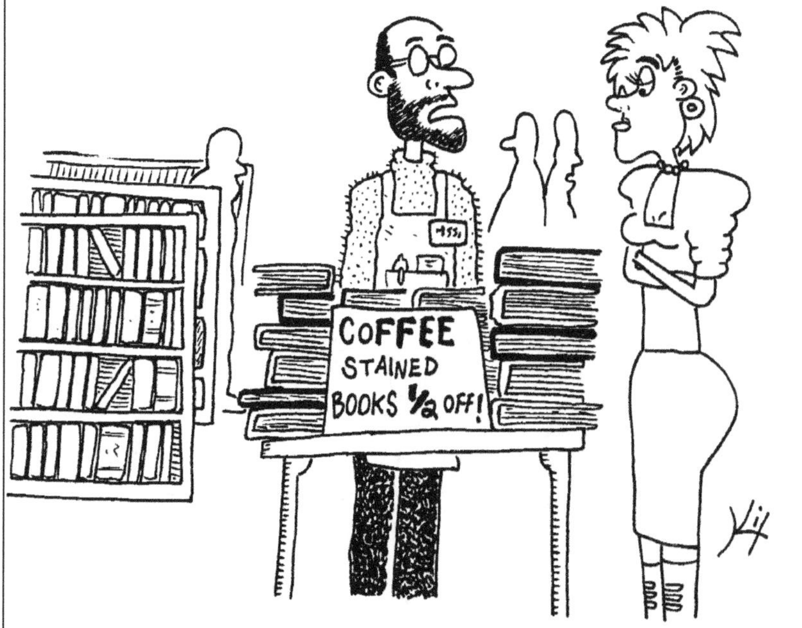
COFFEE
STAINED
BOOKS ½ OFF!

"I dunno, Clarise.... this combination coffee shop - bookstore isn't working out exactly like I planned."

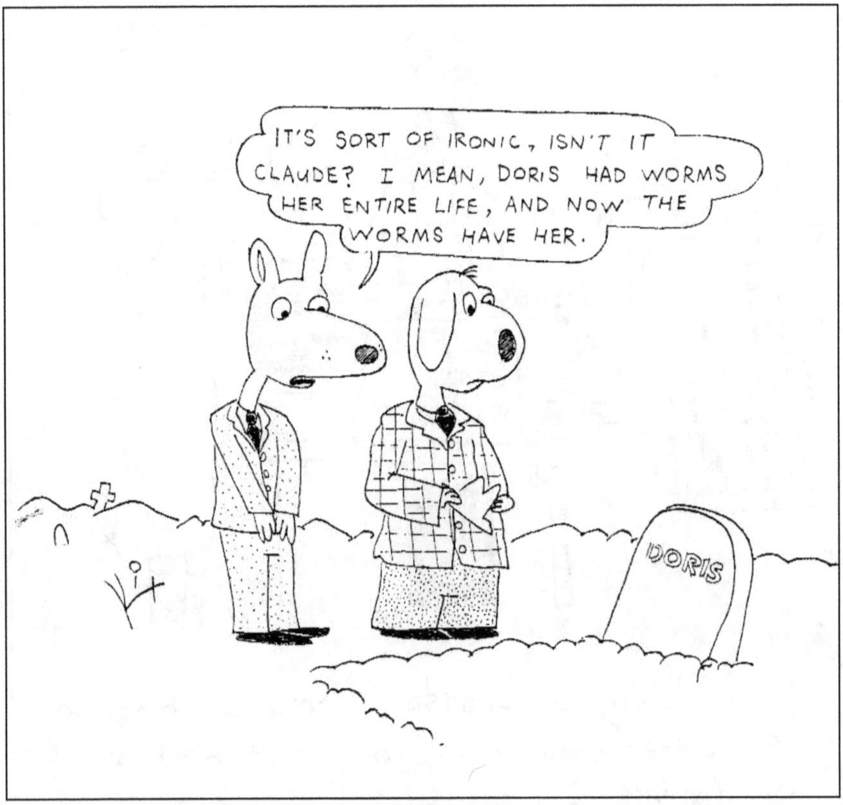
IT'S SORT OF IRONIC, ISN'T IT CLAUDE? I MEAN, DORIS HAD WORMS HER ENTIRE LIFE, AND NOW THE WORMS HAVE HER.
DORIS

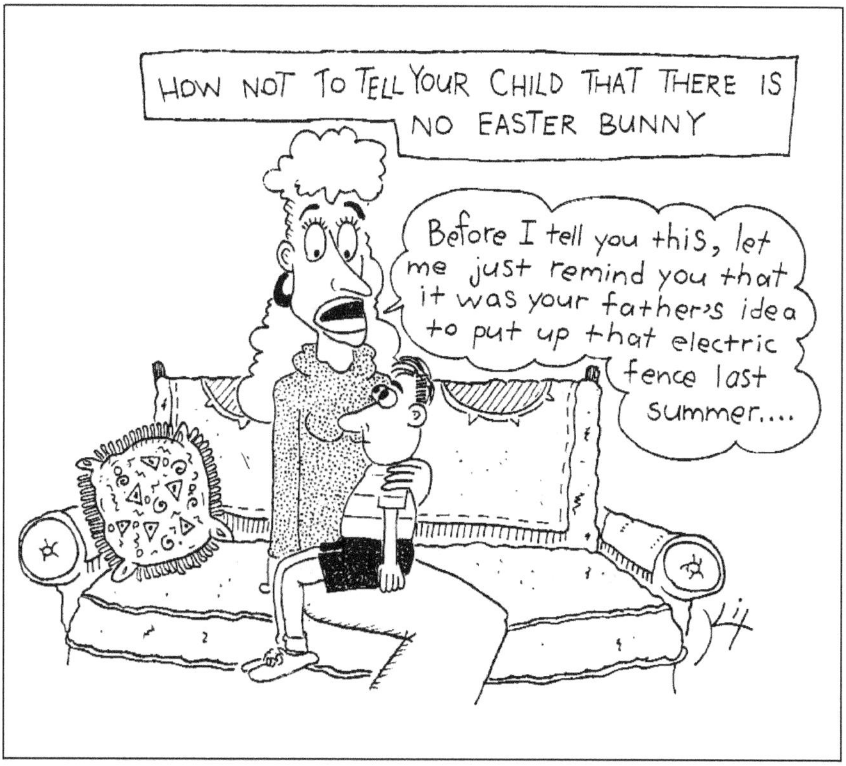
HOW NOT TO TELL YOUR CHILD THAT THERE IS NO EASTER BUNNY
Before I tell you this, let me just remind you that it was your father's idea to put up that electric fence last summer....

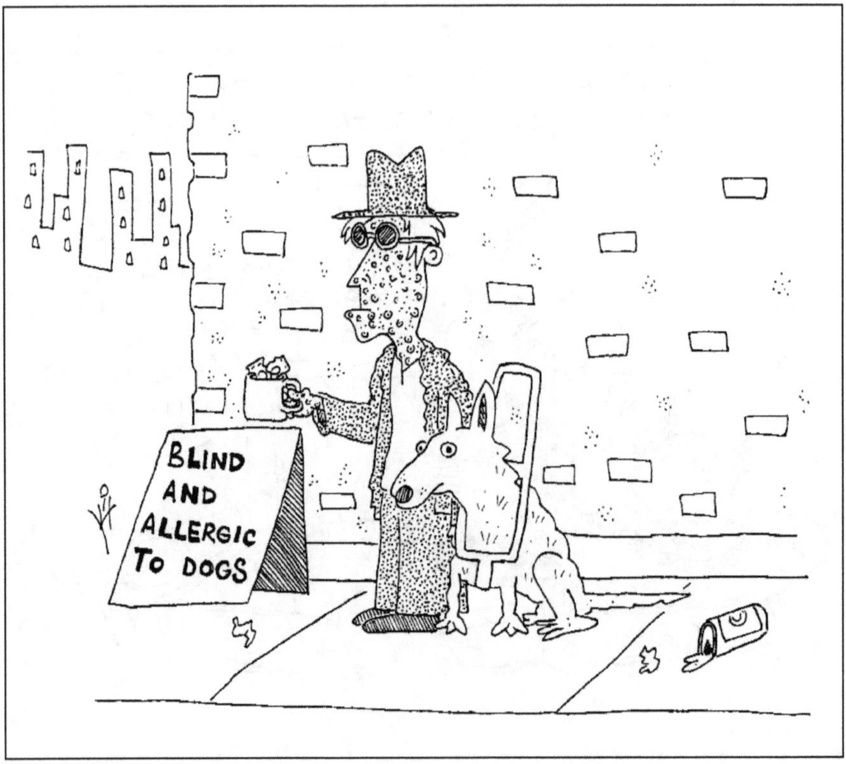
BLIND
AND
ALLERGIC
TO DOGS

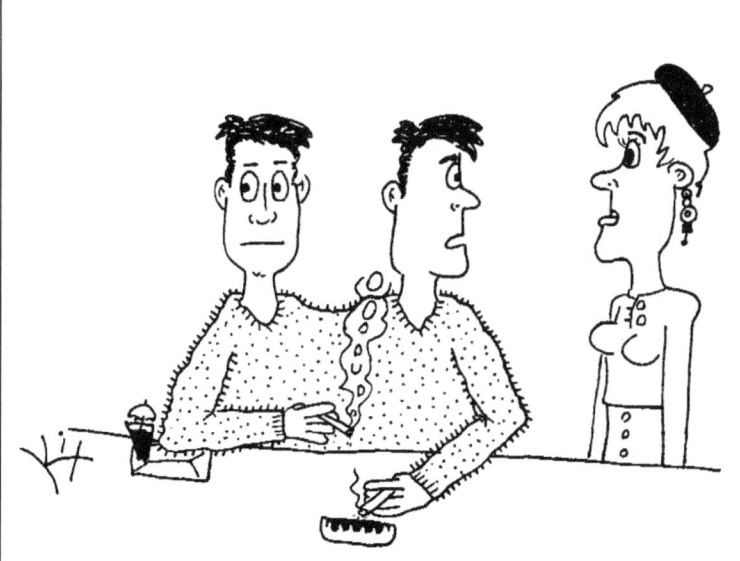

"I almost quit once, but then figured, 'why bother?'; his second-hand smoke was killing me anyway."

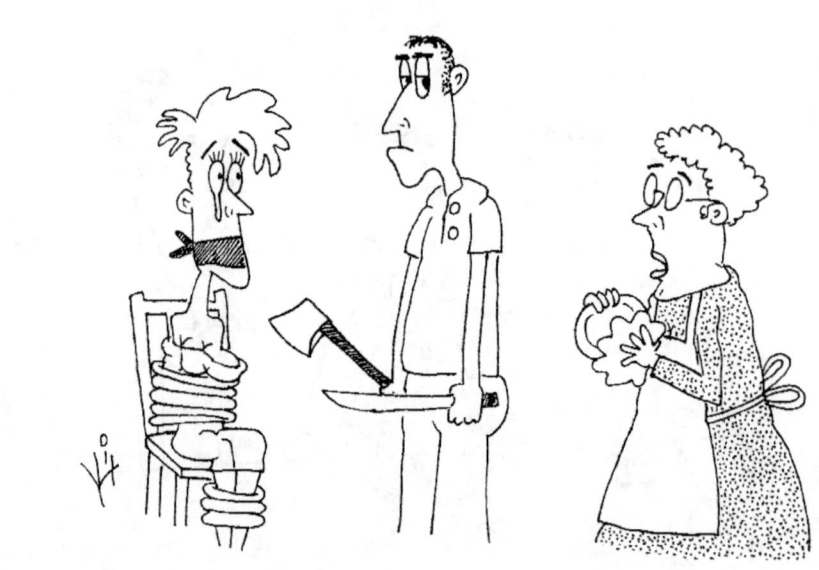

"The ritualistic serial killing I don't mind so much Ricky, but couldn't you bring home some nice girls instead of these tramps?"

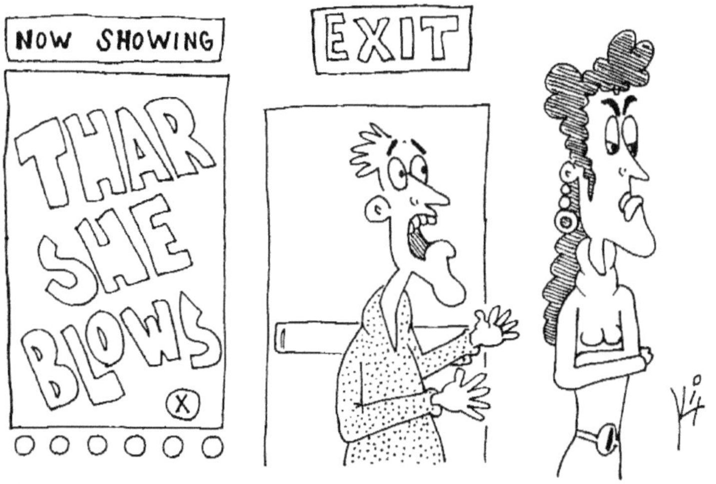
NOW SHOWING
THAR SHE BLOWS
X
EXIT

"HONEY, I SWEAR TO GOD, I THOUGHT THAT IT WAS A MOVIE ABOUT WHALES!"

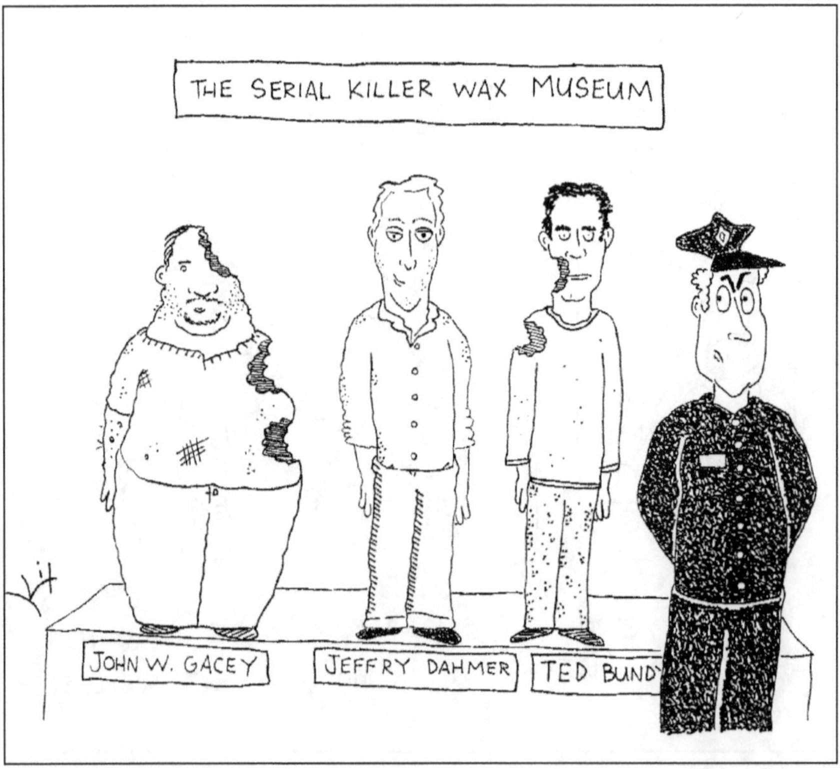
THE SERIAL KILLER WAX MUSEUM
JOHN W. GACEY
JEFFRY DAHMER
TED BUNDY

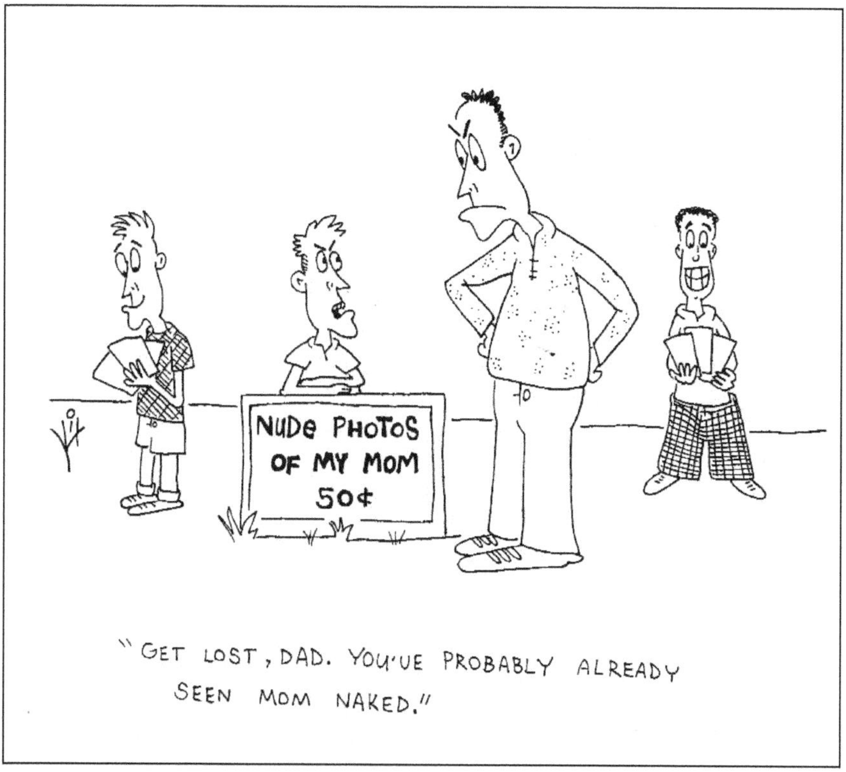
NUDE PHOTOS
OF MY MOM
50¢

"GET LOST, DAD. YOU'VE PROBABLY ALREADY SEEN MOM NAKED."

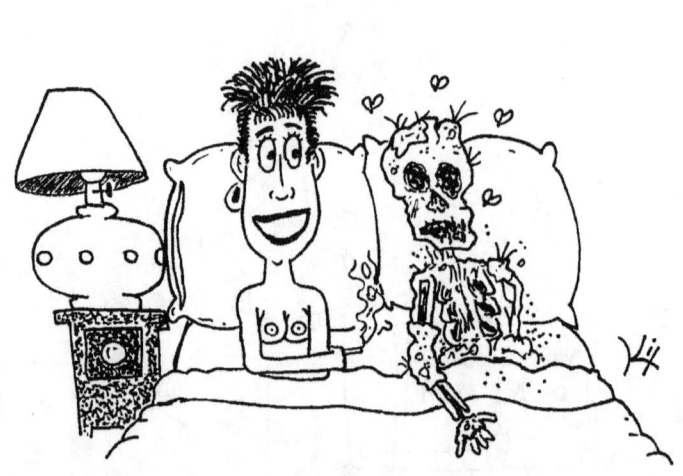

"I hope you realize that I usually don't sleep with a person on the first date. It's just that you're decomposing so quickly, I figured I shouldn't waste any time."

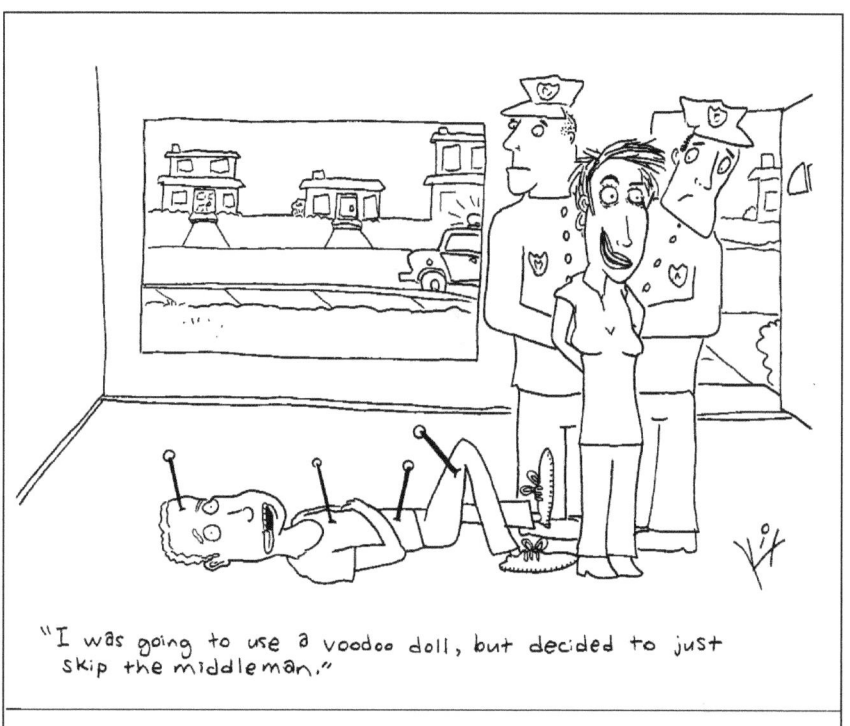

"I was going to use a voodoo doll, but decided to just skip the middleman."

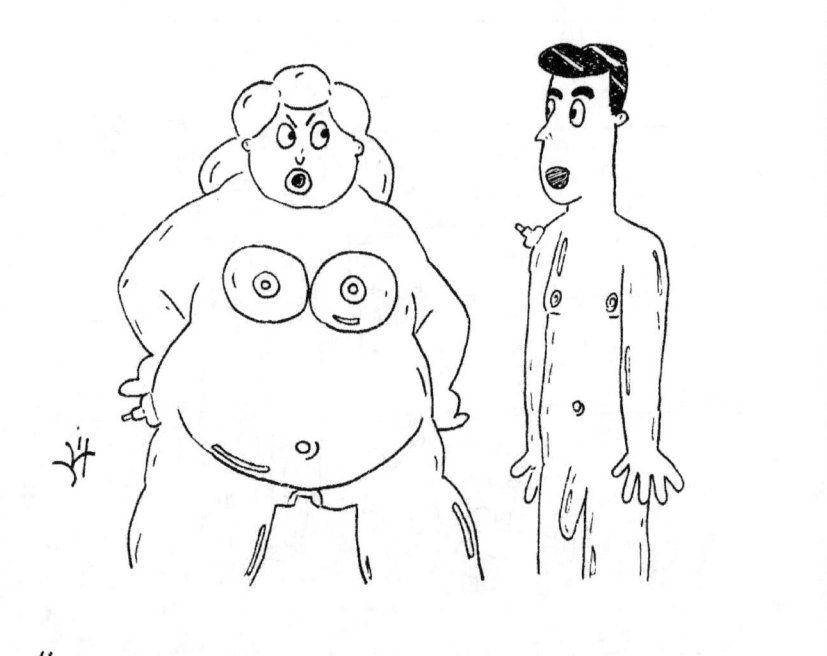

"No offense honey, but I think that maybe you need to lose a little air."

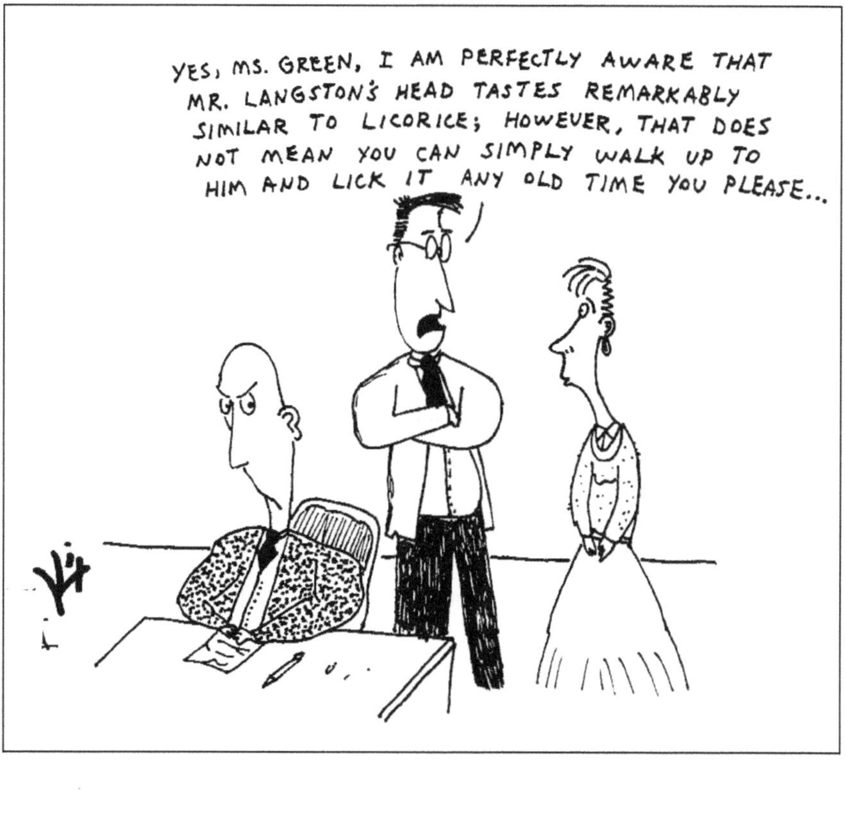
YES, MS. GREEN, I AM PERFECTLY AWARE THAT MR. LANGSTON'S HEAD TASTES REMARKABLY SIMILAR TO LICORICE; HOWEVER, THAT DOES NOT MEAN YOU CAN SIMPLY WALK UP TO HIM AND LICK IT ANY OLD TIME YOU PLEASE...

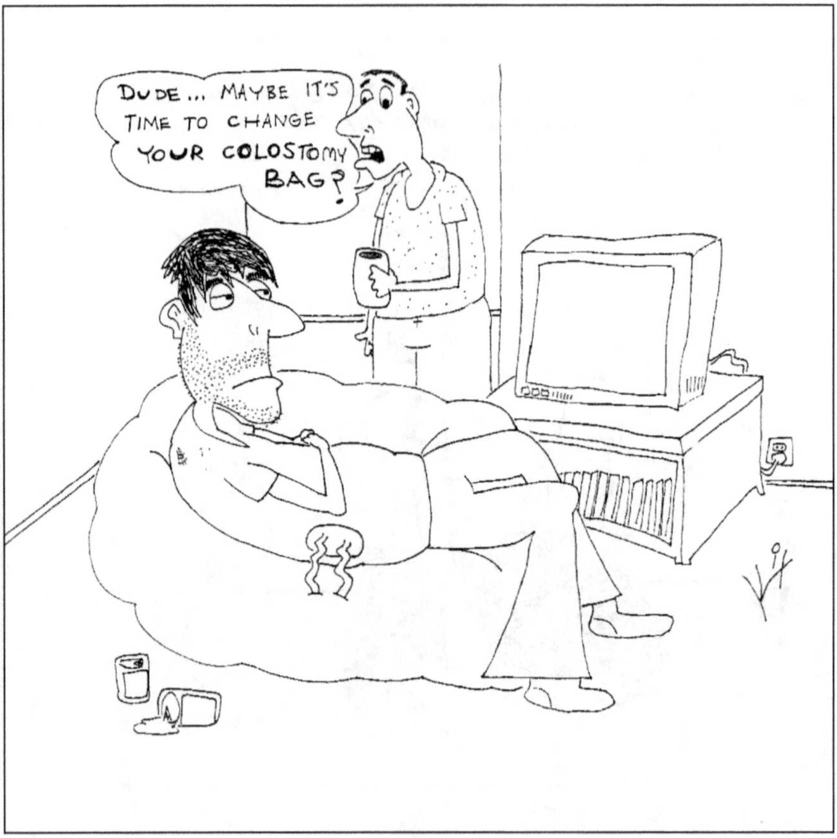
DUDE... MAYBE IT'S TIME TO CHANGE YOUR COLOSTOMY BAG?

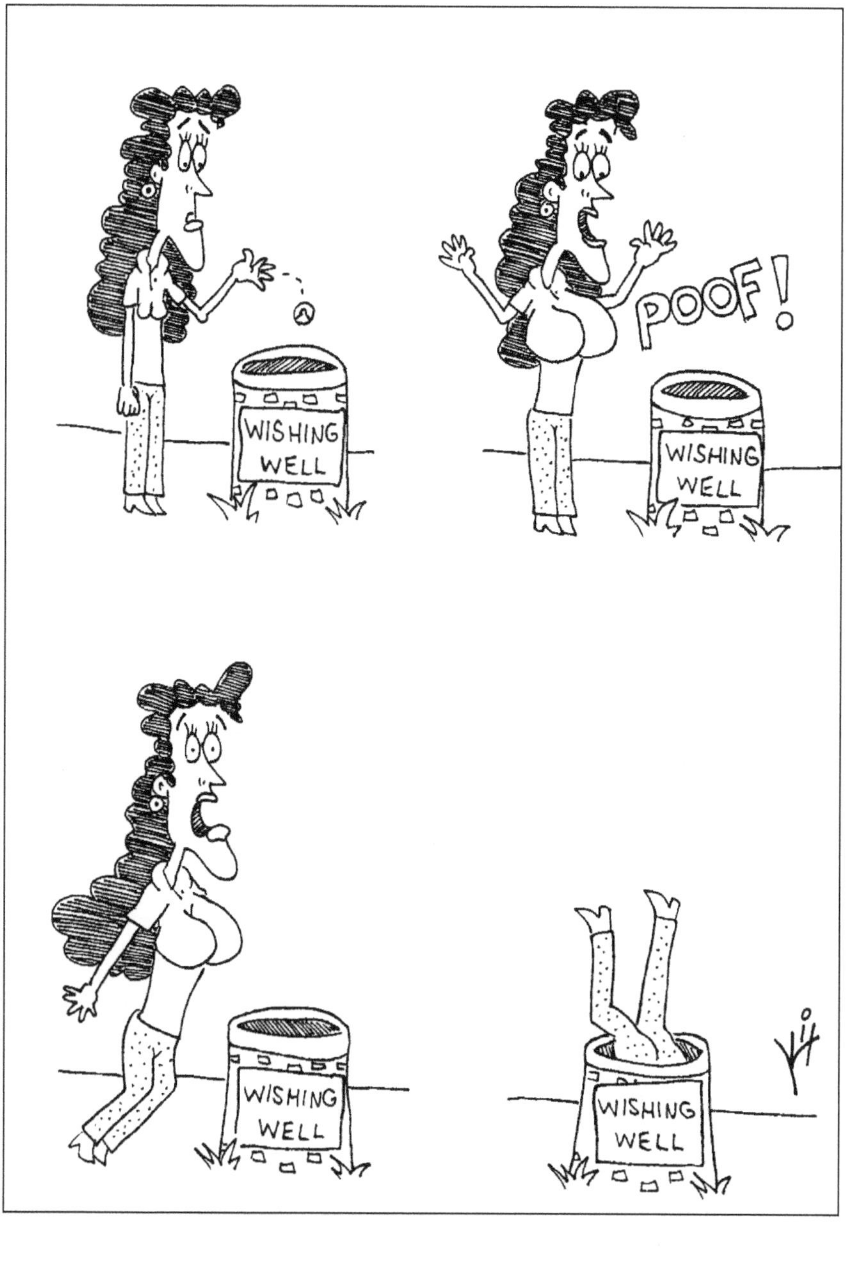
WISHING WELL
POOF!
WISHING WELL
WISHING WELL
WISHING WELL

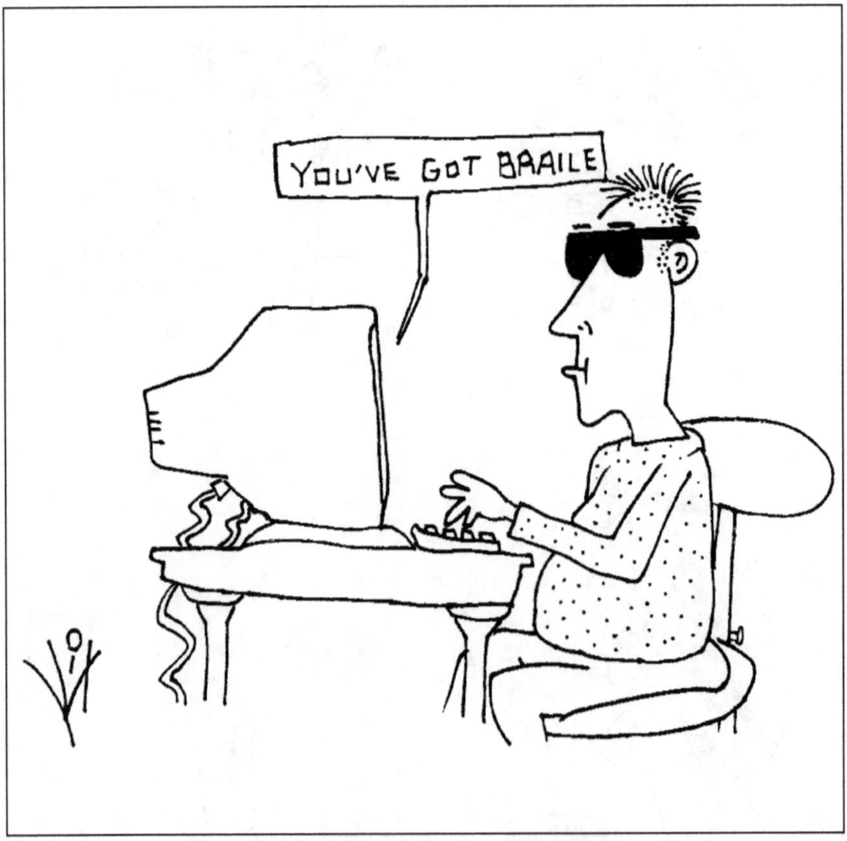
YOU'VE GOT BRAILE

GOTHMOPOLITAN
Price: Your Parent's Love
PENTAGRAMS OF FAT: The new Goth Diet!
THE THIRD DATE: TOO SOON TO DRINK EACH OTHER'S BLOOD?
Absinthe Makes the heart grow fonder
"WHOSE UN-INVERTED CROSS IS THIS?!" How To Tell if Your Man is Cheating on You With a Christian

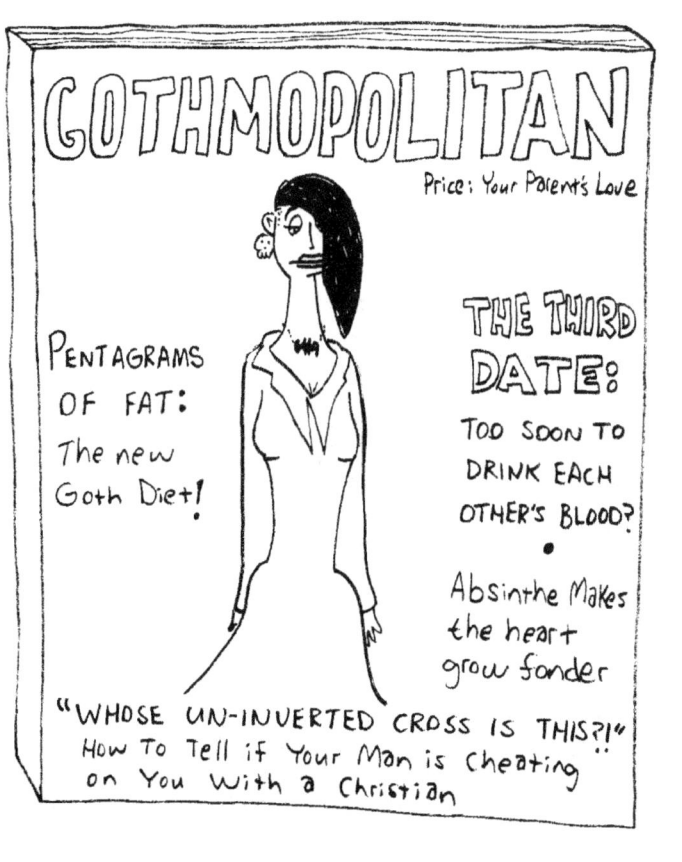

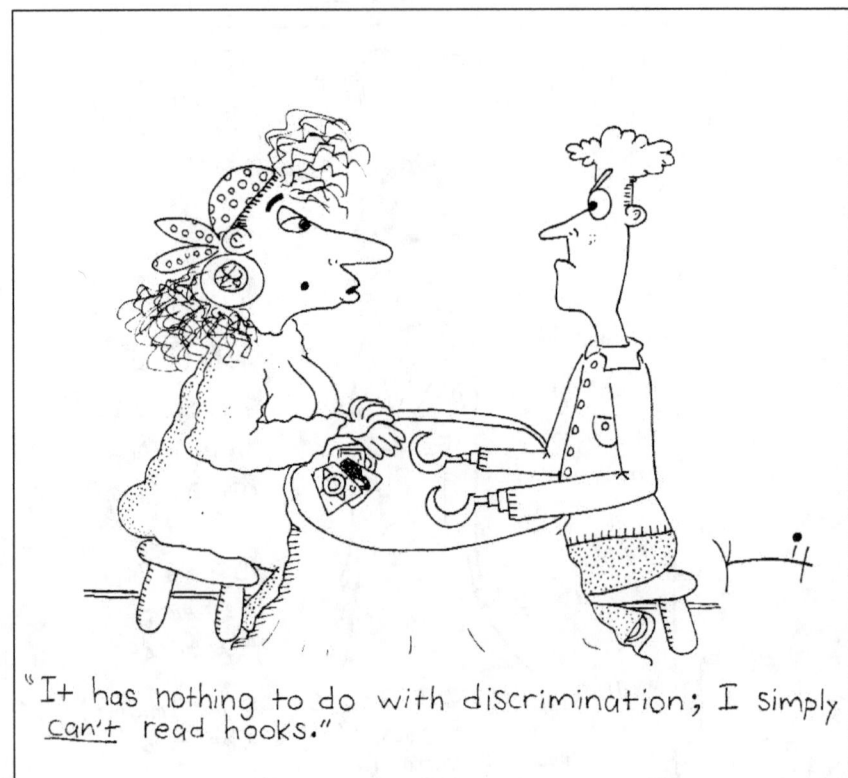

"It has nothing to do with discrimination; I simply can't read hooks."

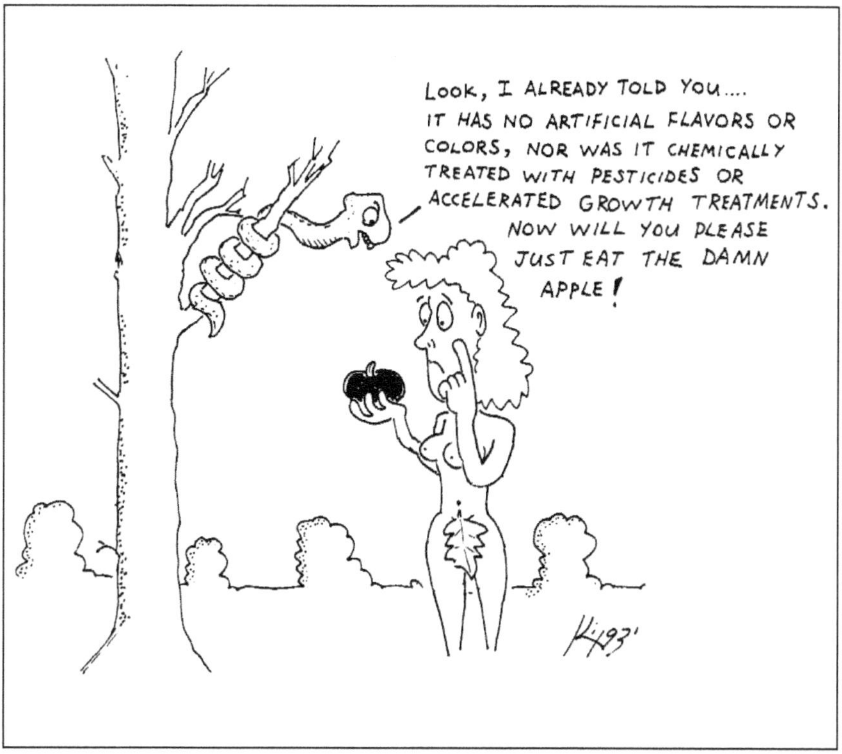
LOOK, I ALREADY TOLD YOU....
IT HAS NO ARTIFICIAL FLAVORS OR COLORS, NOR WAS IT CHEMICALLY TREATED WITH PESTICIDES OR ACCELERATED GROWTH TREATMENTS. NOW WILL YOU PLEASE JUST EAT THE DAMN APPLE!

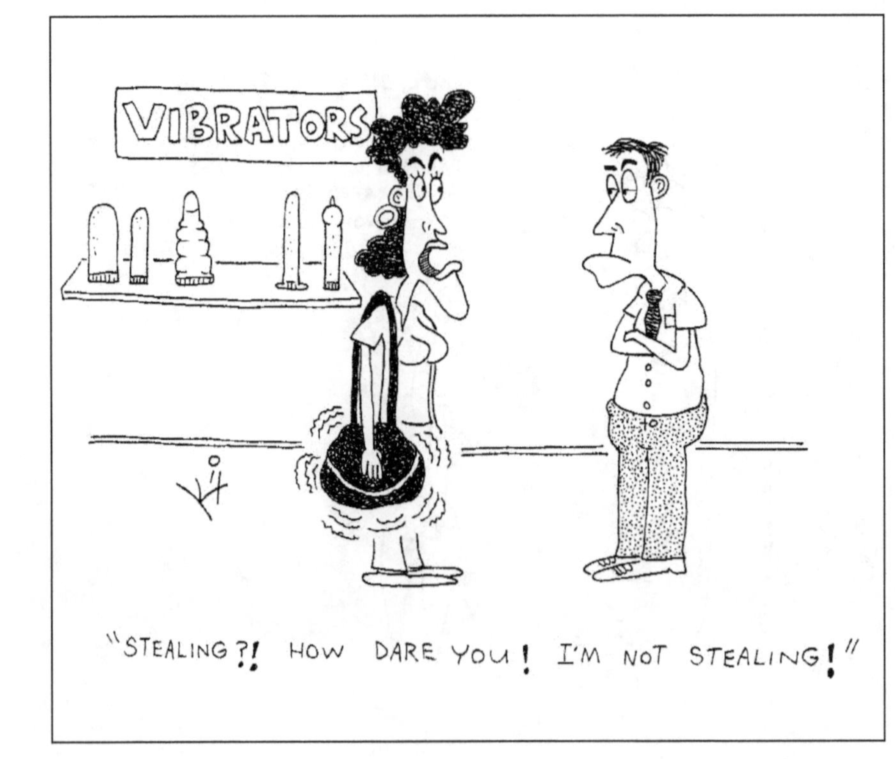
VIBRATORS

"STEALING?! HOW DARE YOU! I'M NOT STEALING!"

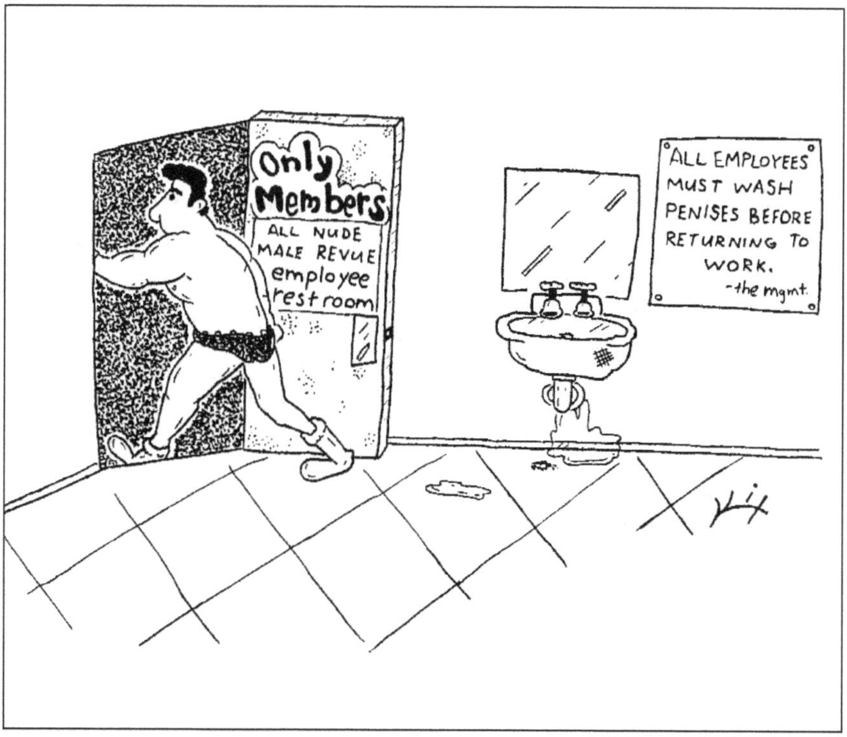
Only Members
ALL NUDE MALE REVUE employee restroom
ALL EMPLOYEES MUST WASH PENISES BEFORE RETURNING TO WORK.
-the mgmt.

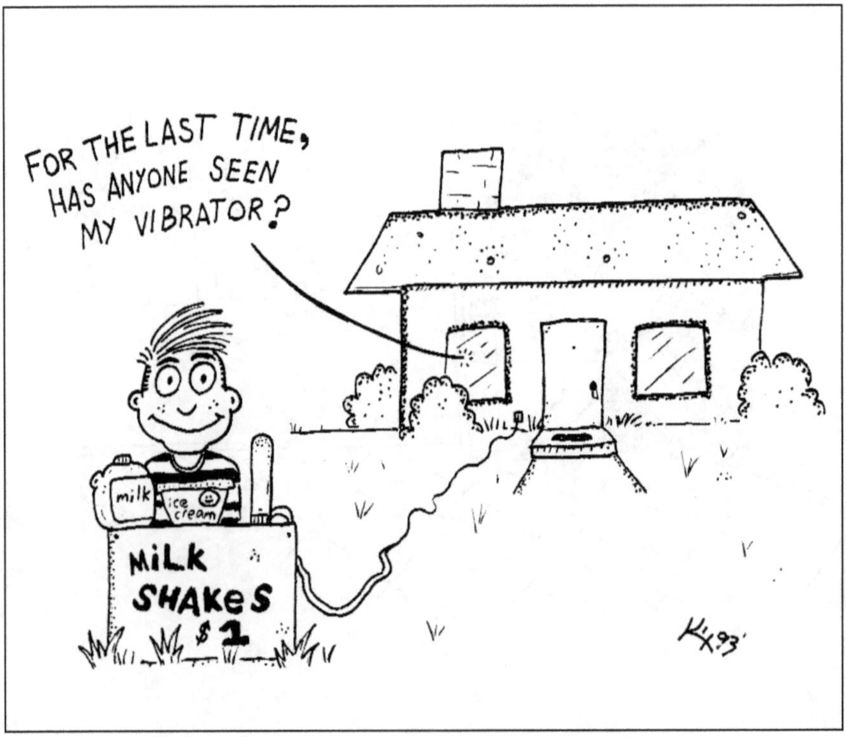
FOR THE LAST TIME, HAS ANYONE SEEN MY VIBRATOR?
milk
ice cream
MILK SHAKES $1
KK '93

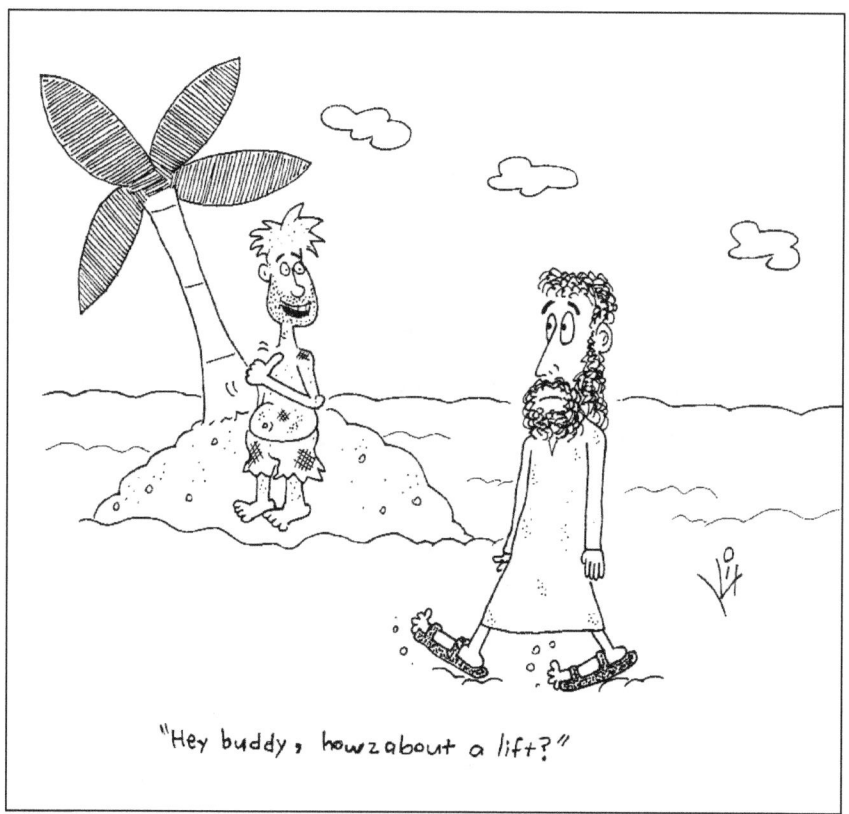

"Hey buddy, howzabout a lift?"

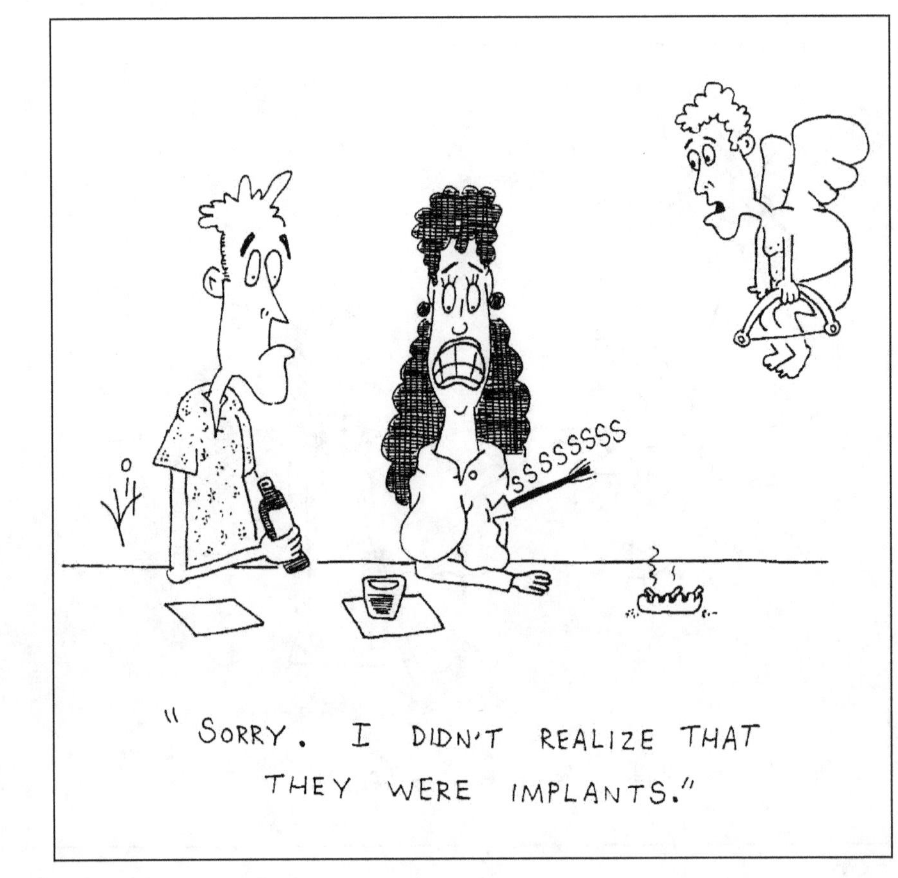
SSSSSSSS

"SORRY. I DIDN'T REALIZE THAT THEY WERE IMPLANTS."

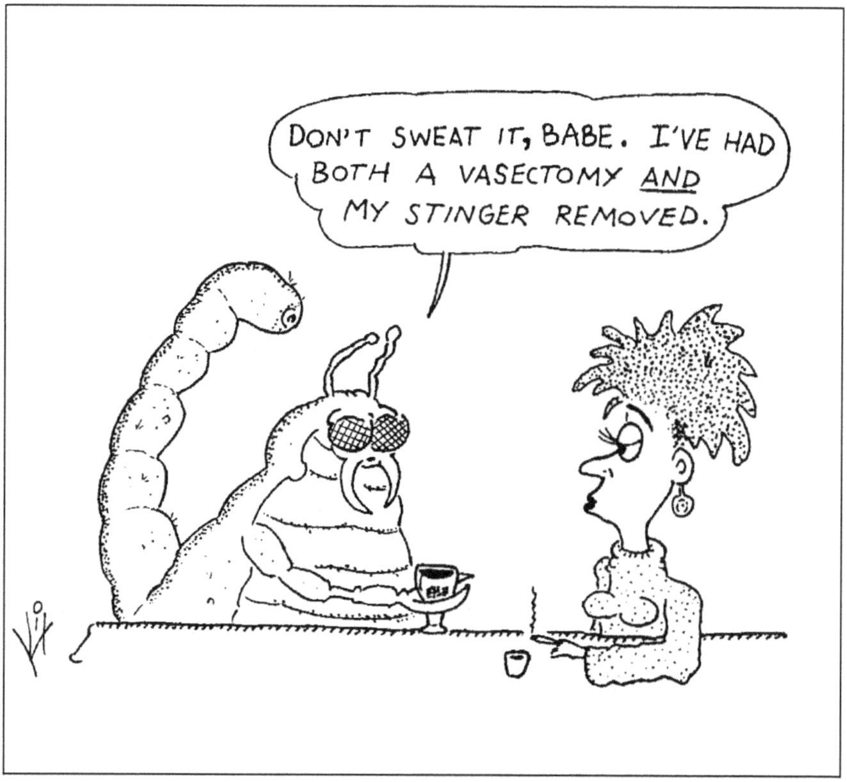
DON'T SWEAT IT, BABE. I'VE HAD BOTH A VASECTOMY AND MY STINGER REMOVED.

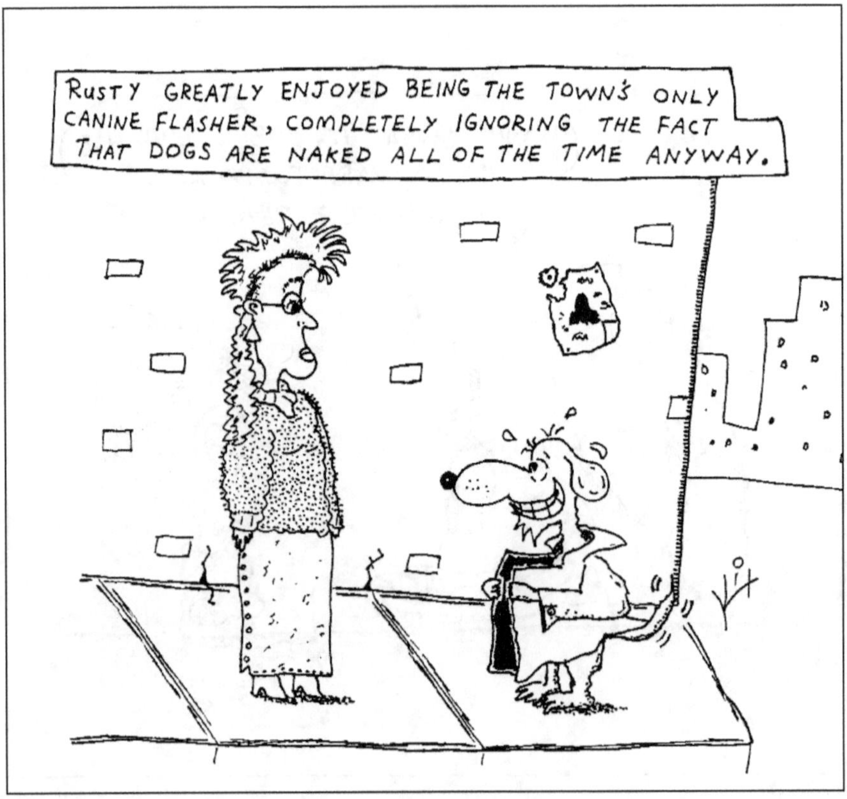
RUSTY GREATLY ENJOYED BEING THE TOWN'S ONLY CANINE FLASHER, COMPLETELY IGNORING THE FACT THAT DOGS ARE NAKED ALL OF THE TIME ANYWAY.

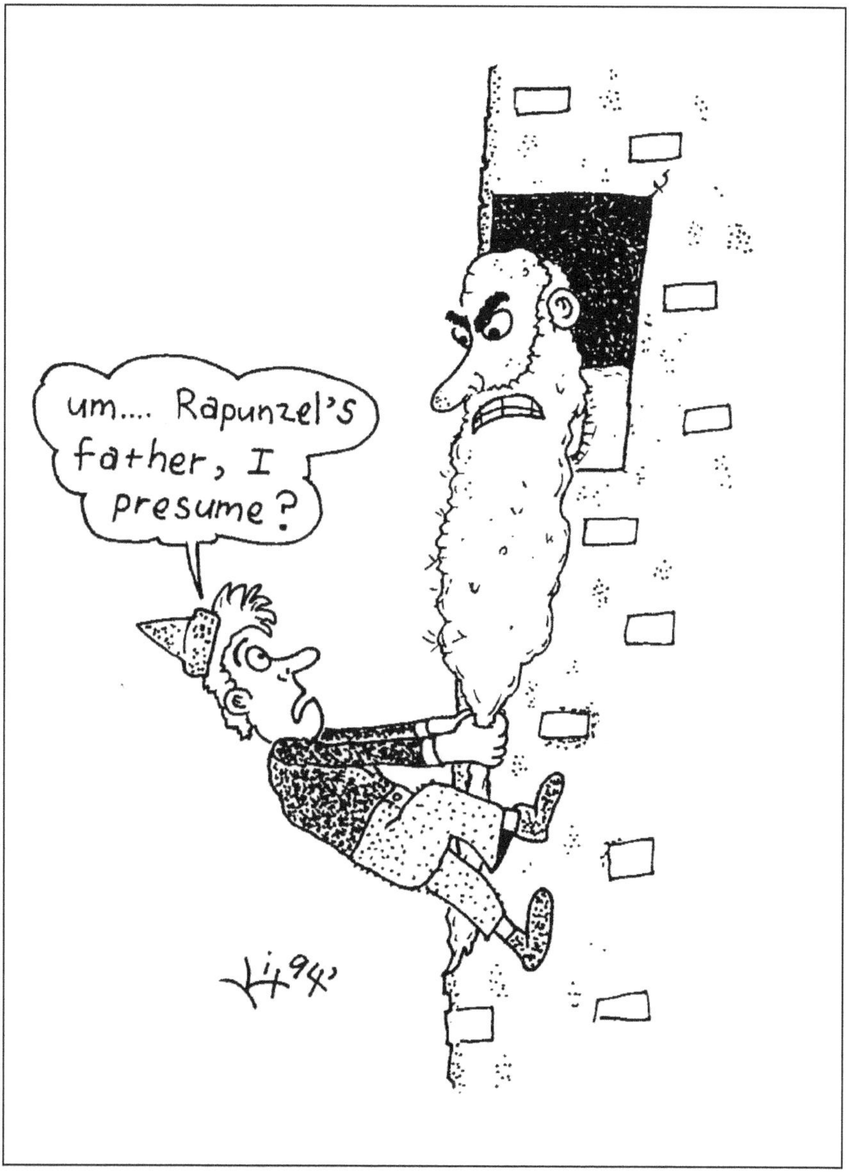
um.... Rapunzel's
father, I
presume?

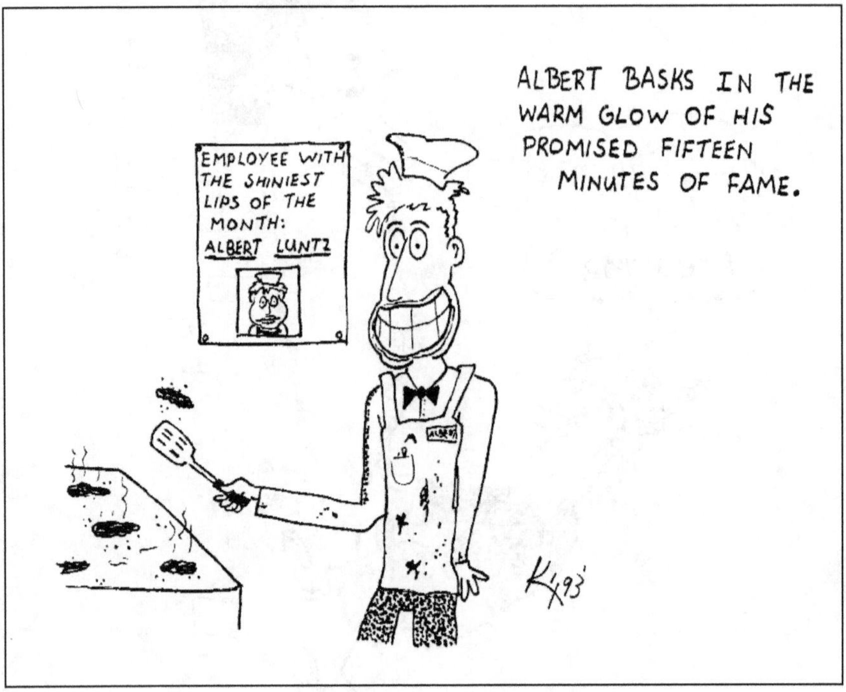
ALBERT BASKS IN THE WARM GLOW OF HIS PROMISED FIFTEEN MINUTES OF FAME.
EMPLOYEE WITH THE SHINIEST LIPS OF THE MONTH: ALBERT LUNTZ
ALBERT
K 93'

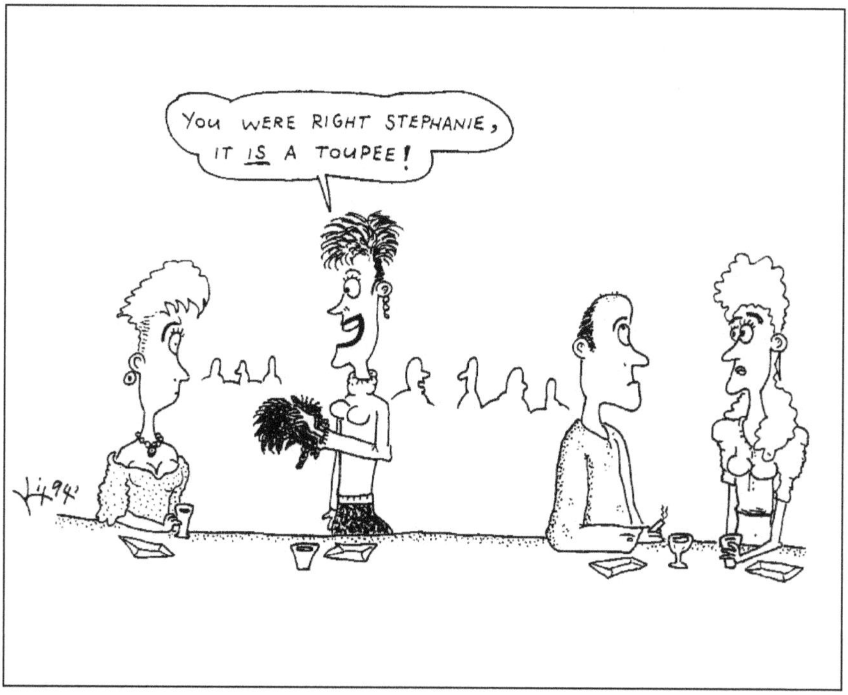
YOU WERE RIGHT STEPHANIE,
IT IS A TOUPEE!

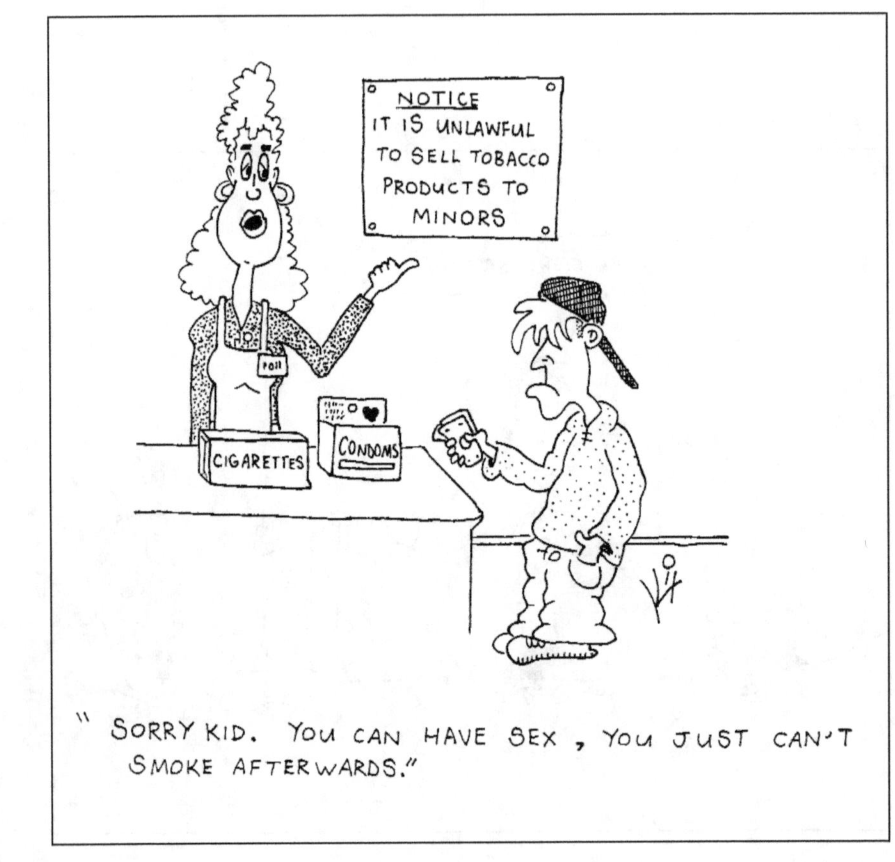
NOTICE
IT IS UNLAWFUL TO SELL TOBACCO PRODUCTS TO MINORS
CIGARETTES
CONDOMS

"SORRY KID. YOU CAN HAVE SEX, YOU JUST CAN'T SMOKE AFTERWARDS."

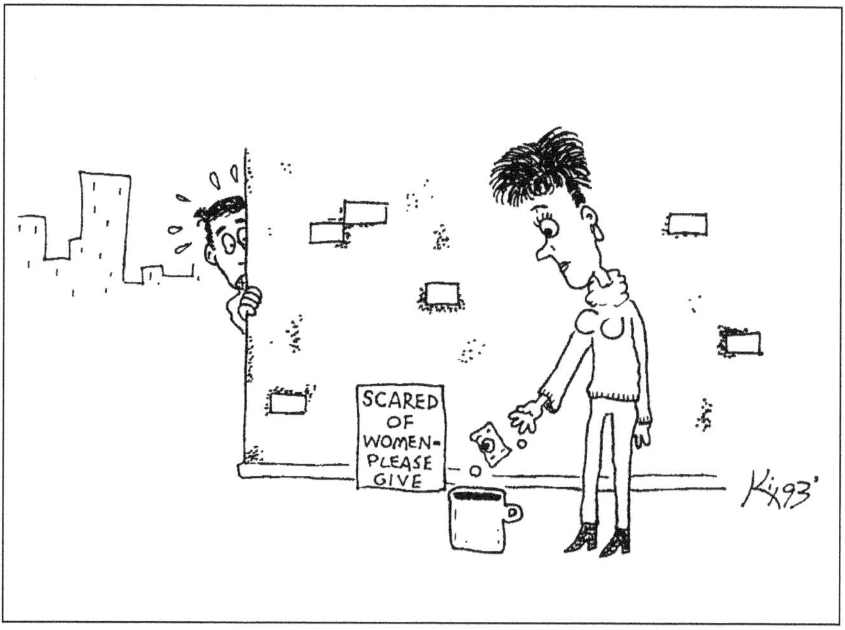
SCARED
OF
WOMEN-
PLEASE
GIVE
Kix93'

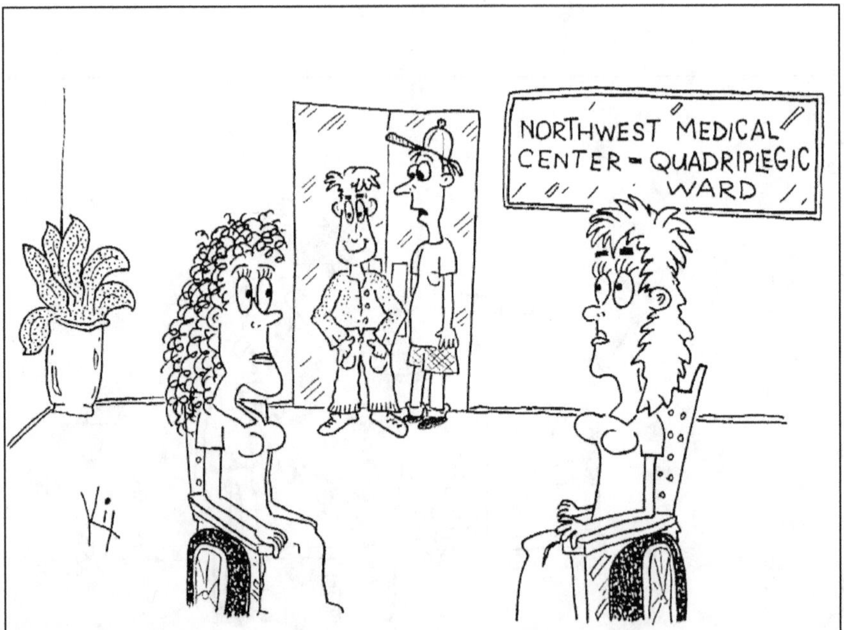
NORTHWEST MEDICAL
CENTER - QUADRIPLEGIC
WARD

"I dunno about this Roy; I thought you said that we were going to fuck any thing that <u>moves</u>."

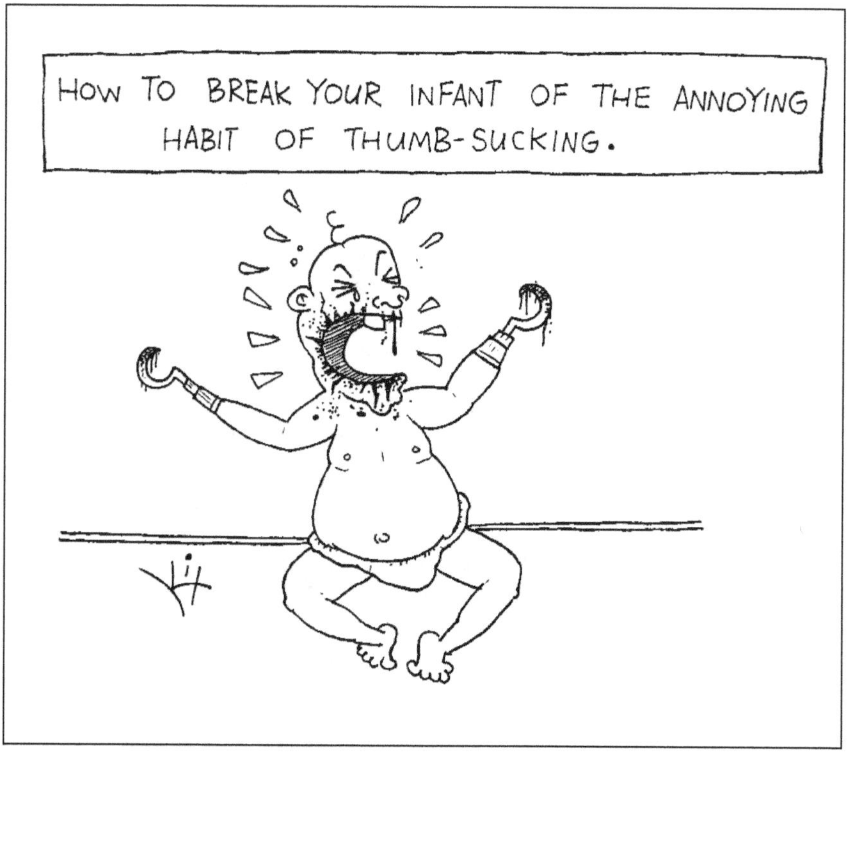
HOW TO BREAK YOUR INFANT OF THE ANNOYING HABIT OF THUMB-SUCKING.

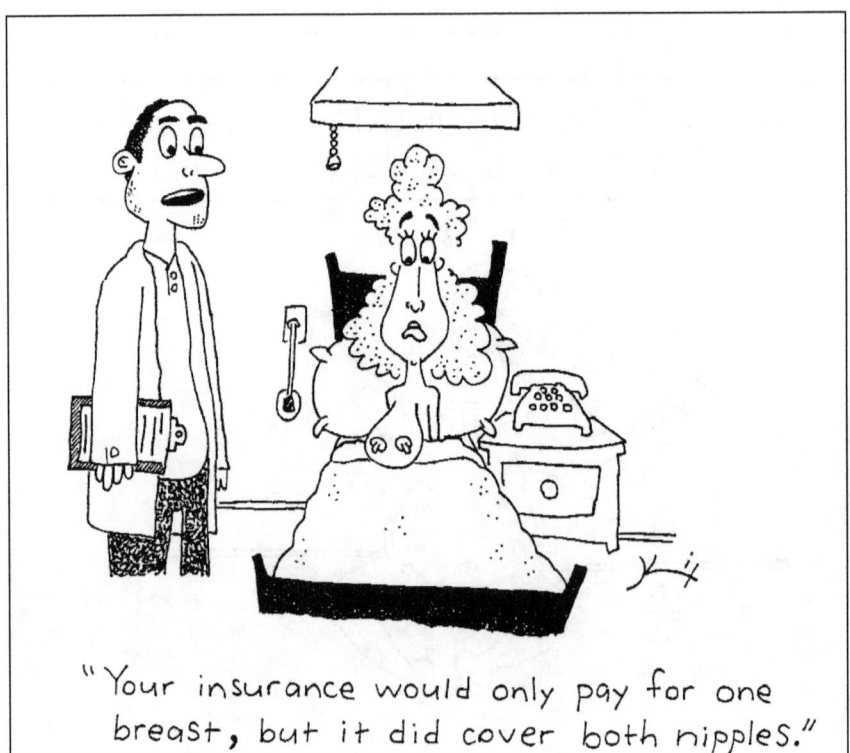

"Your insurance would only pay for one breast, but it did cover both nipples."

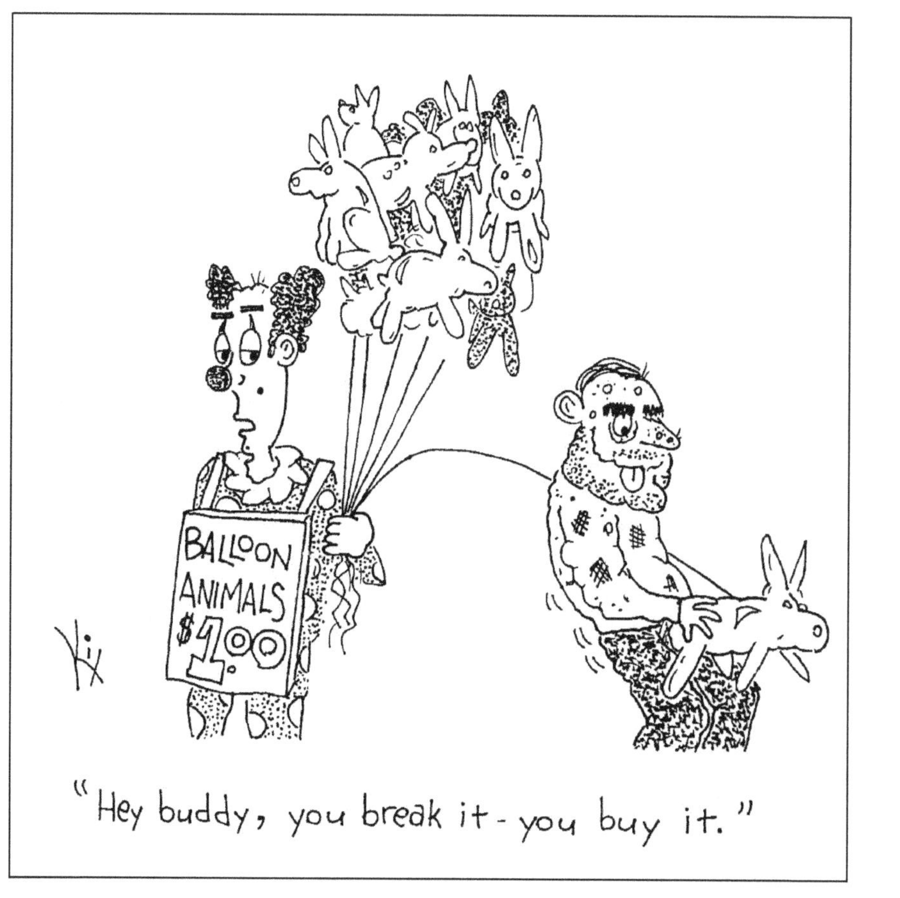
BALLOON
ANIMALS
$1.00

"Hey buddy, you break it - you buy it."

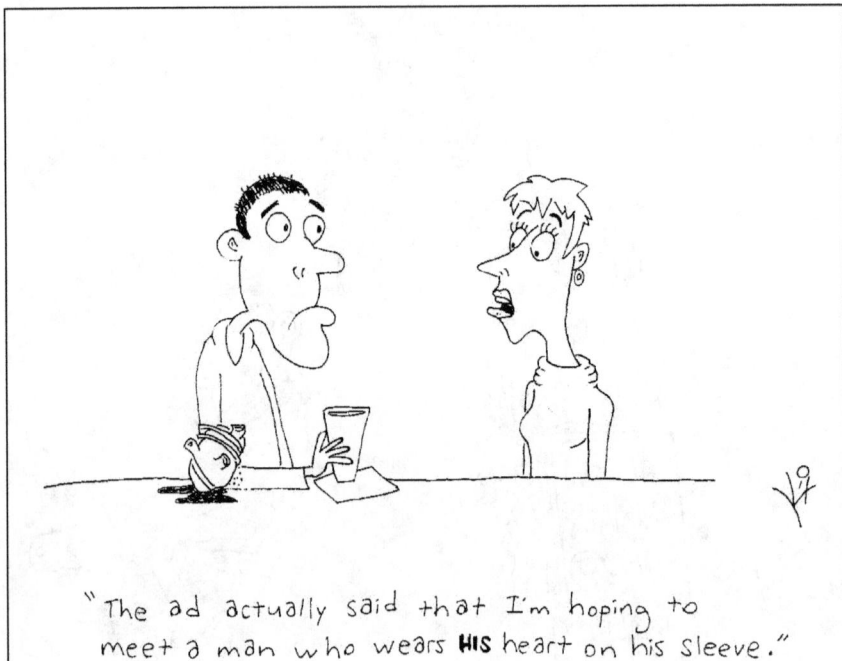

"The ad actually said that I'm hoping to meet a man who wears **HIS** heart on his sleeve."

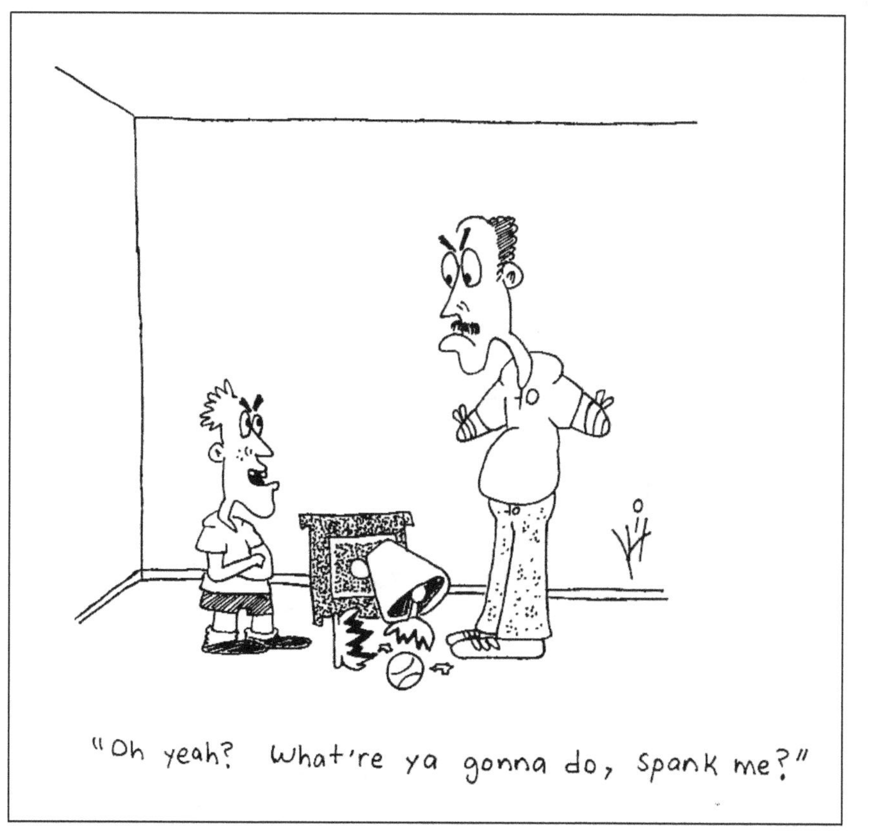

"Oh yeah? What're ya gonna do, spank me?"

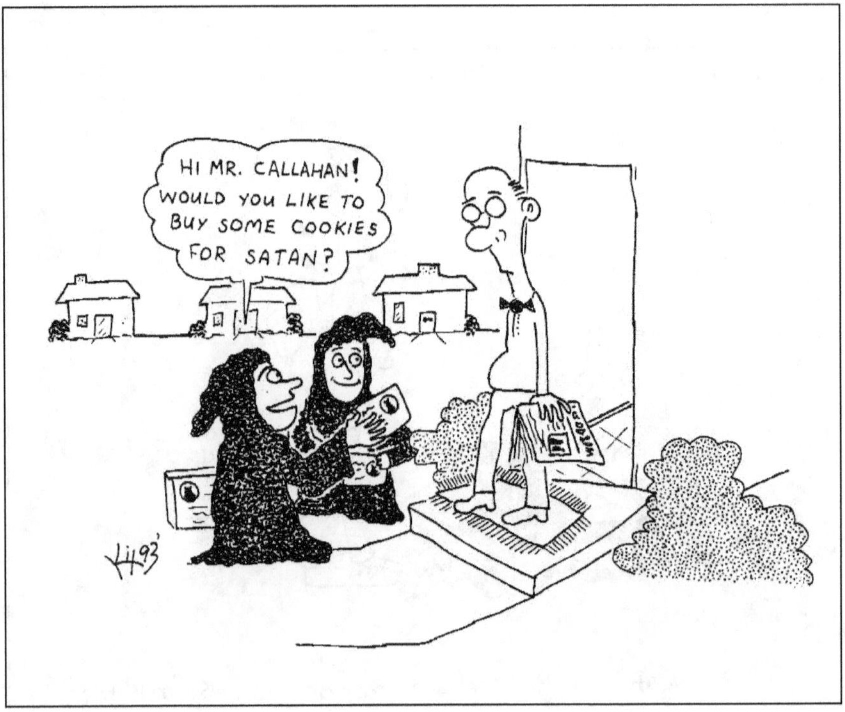
HI MR. CALLAHAN! WOULD YOU LIKE TO BUY SOME COOKIES FOR SATAN?

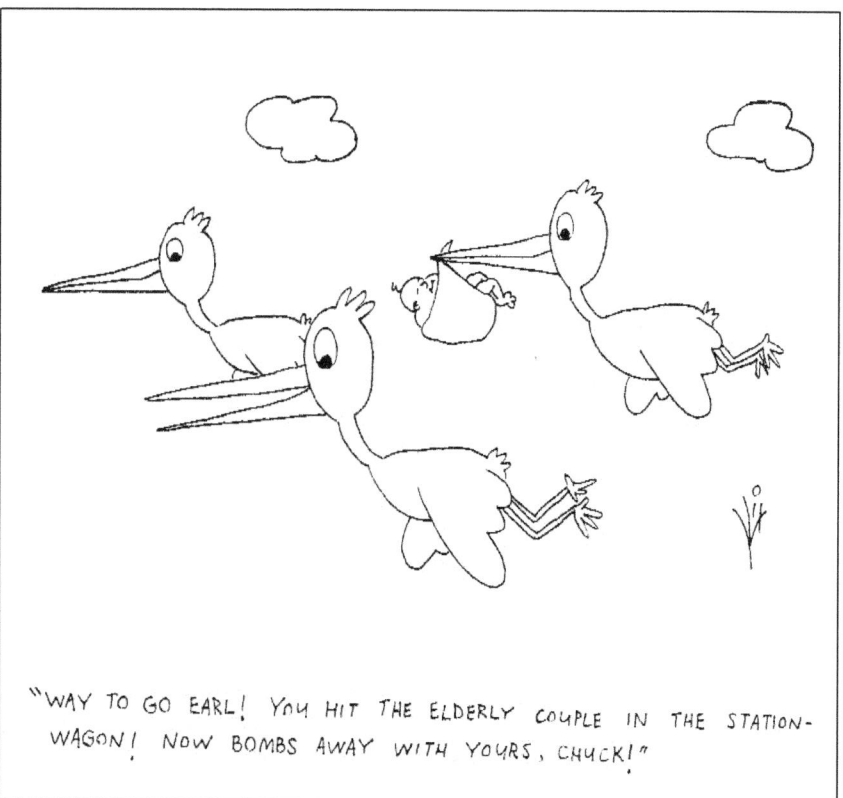

"WAY TO GO EARL! YOU HIT THE ELDERLY COUPLE IN THE STATION-WAGON! NOW BOMBS AWAY WITH YOURS, CHUCK!"

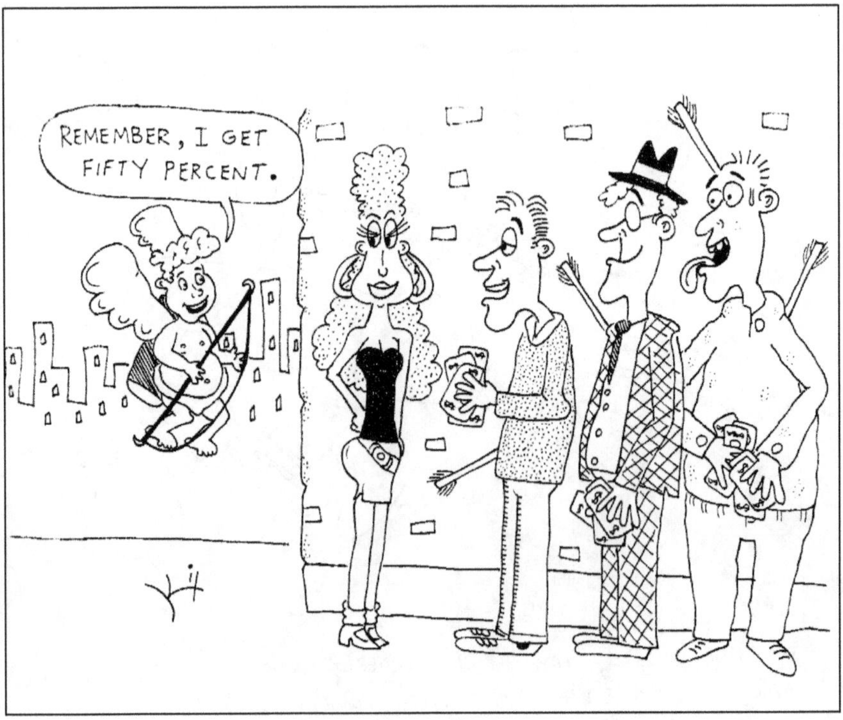
REMEMBER, I GET FIFTY PERCENT.

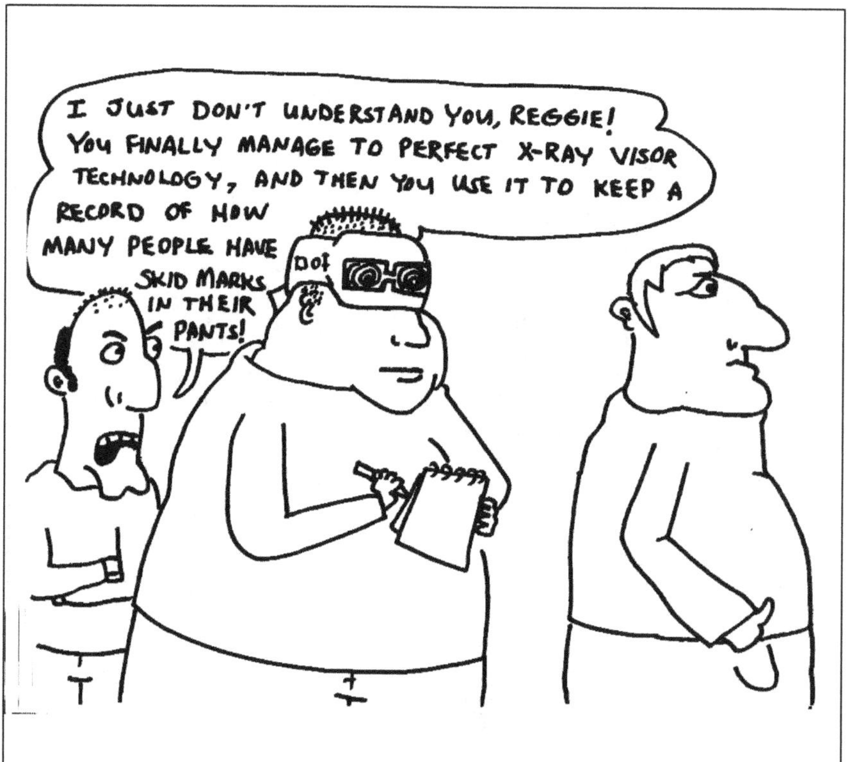
I JUST DON'T UNDERSTAND YOU, REGGIE! YOU FINALLY MANAGE TO PERFECT X-RAY VISOR TECHNOLOGY, AND THEN YOU USE IT TO KEEP A RECORD OF HOW MANY PEOPLE HAVE SKID MARKS IN THEIR PANTS!

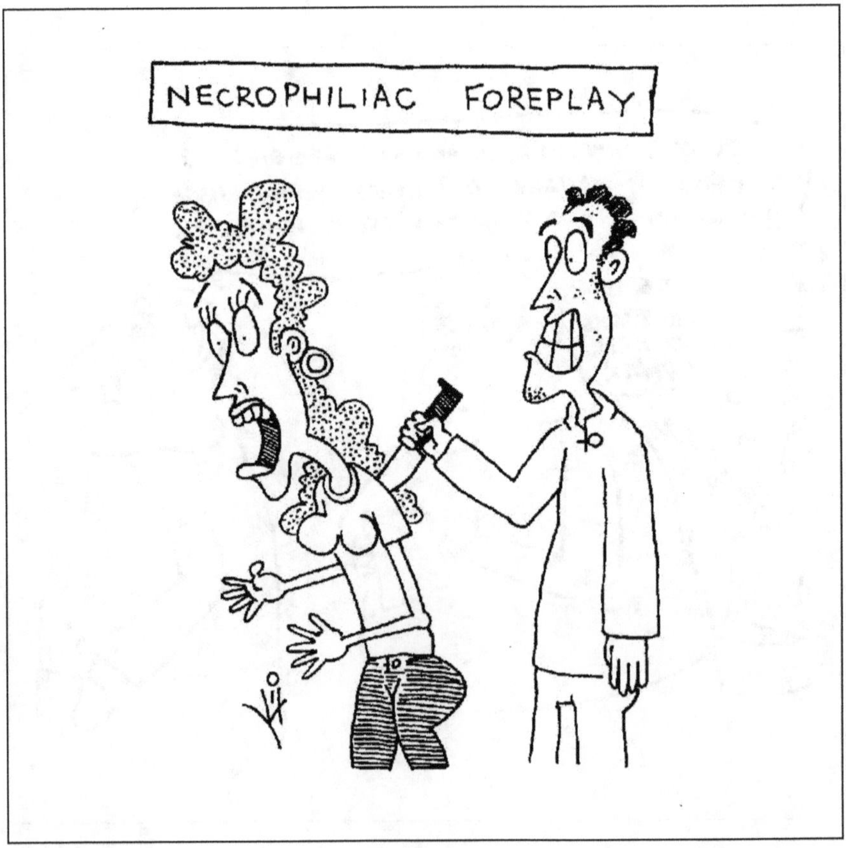
NECROPHILIAC FOREPLAY

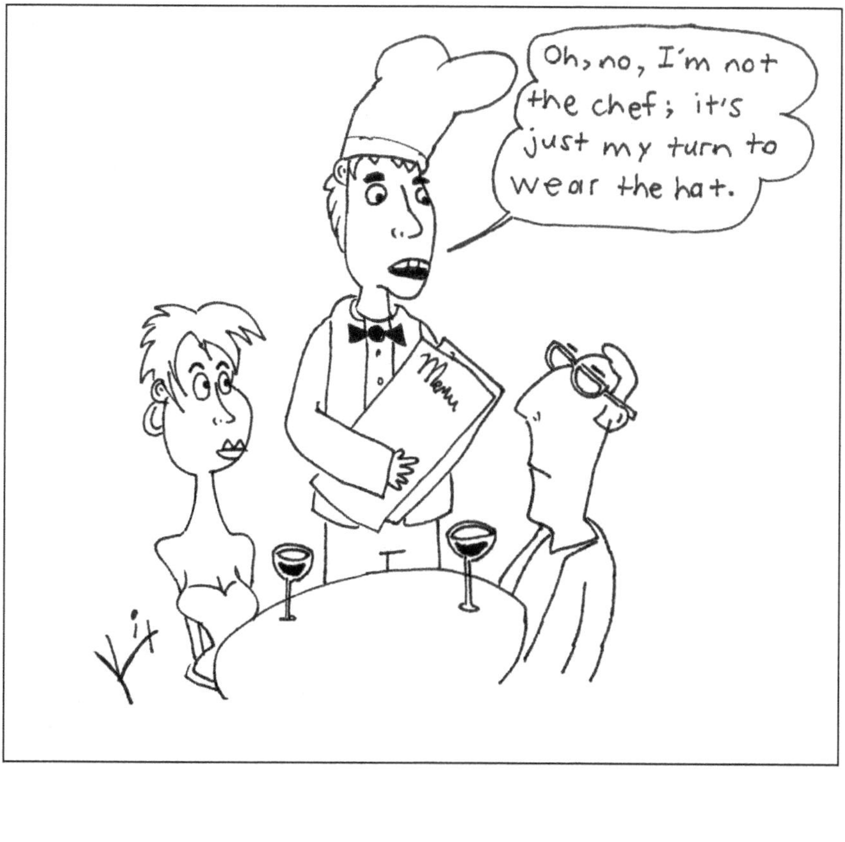
Oh, no, I'm not the chef; it's just my turn to wear the hat.
Menu

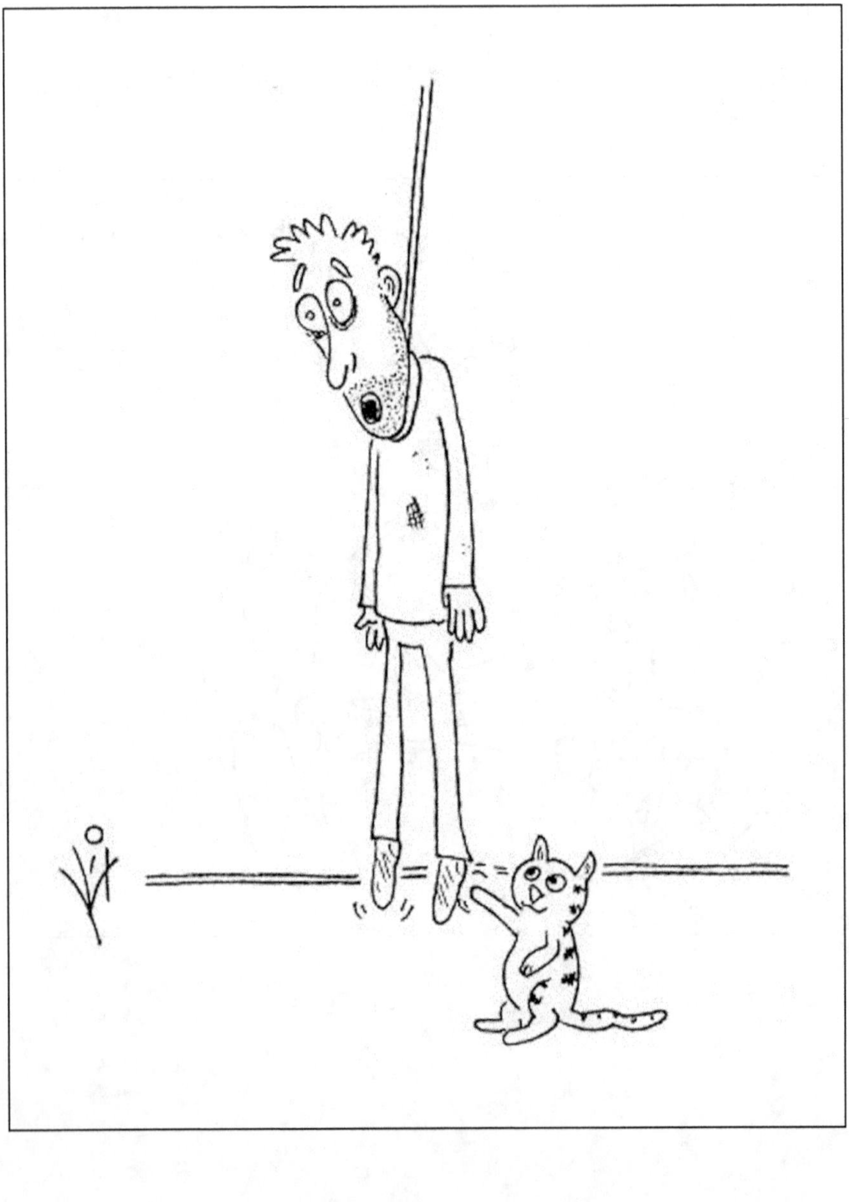

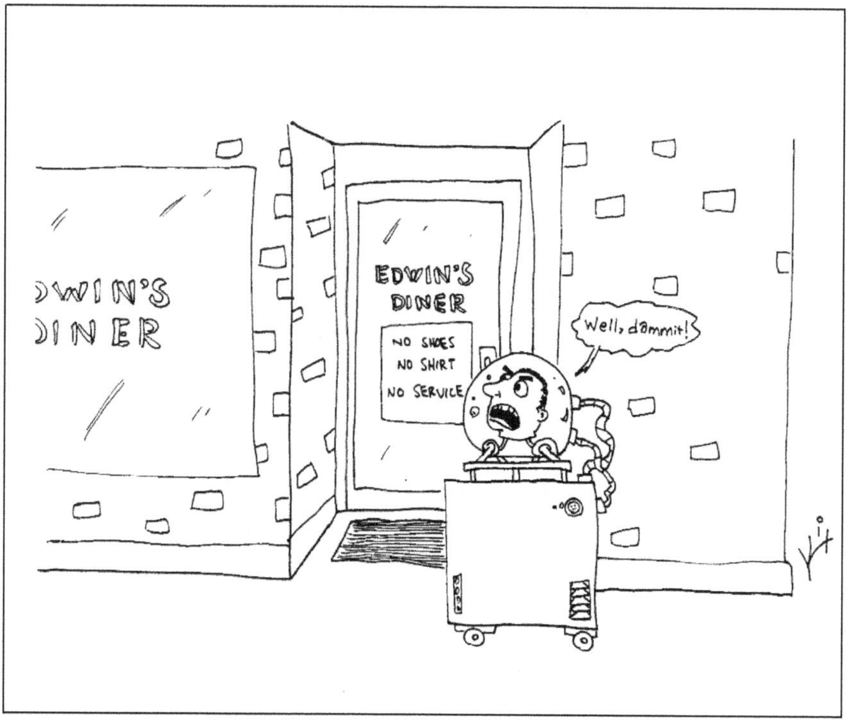
DWIN'S
DINER
EDWIN'S
DINER
NO SHOES
NO SHIRT
NO SERVICE
Well, dammit!

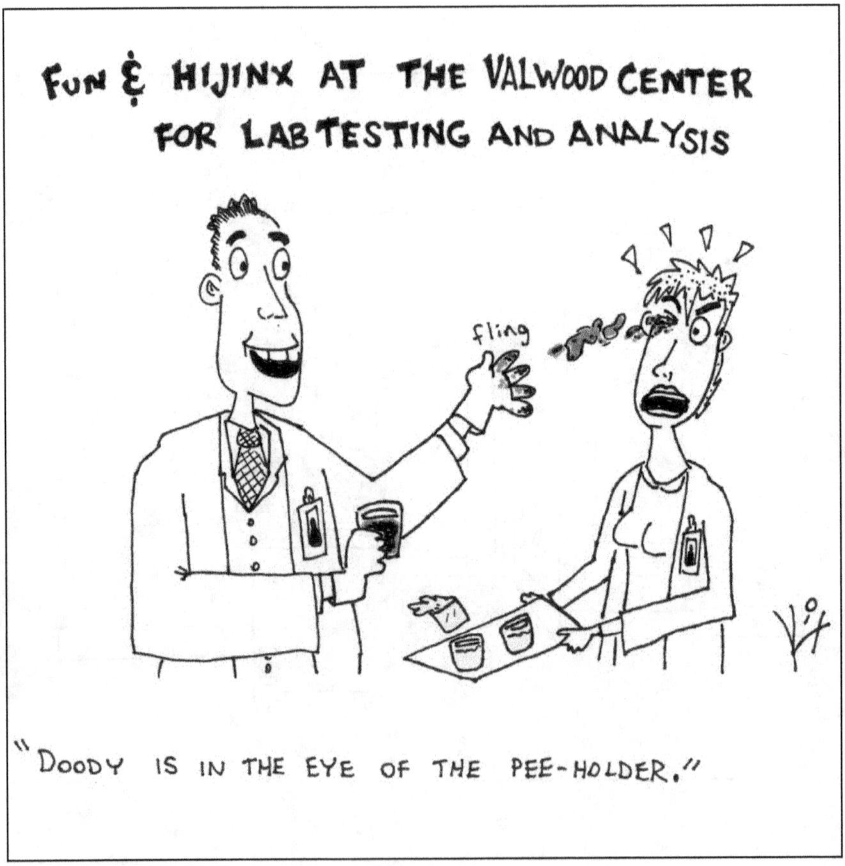
Fun & Hijinx at the Valwood Center for Lab Testing and Analysis
fling

"Doody is in the eye of the pee-holder."

Due to a mix-up at a Waffle-House in Nebraska, Billy wound up with the Pope's hat, and the Pope with Billy's.

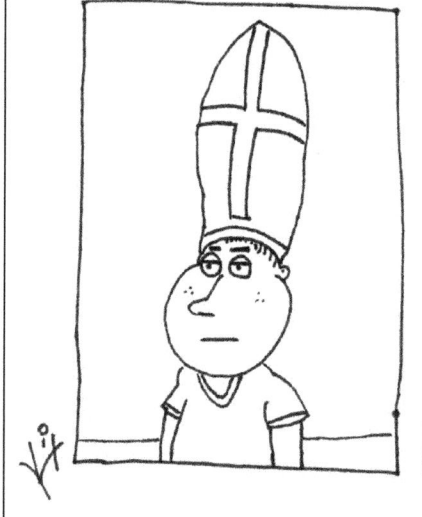
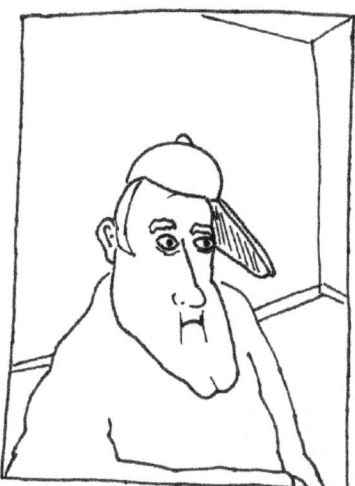

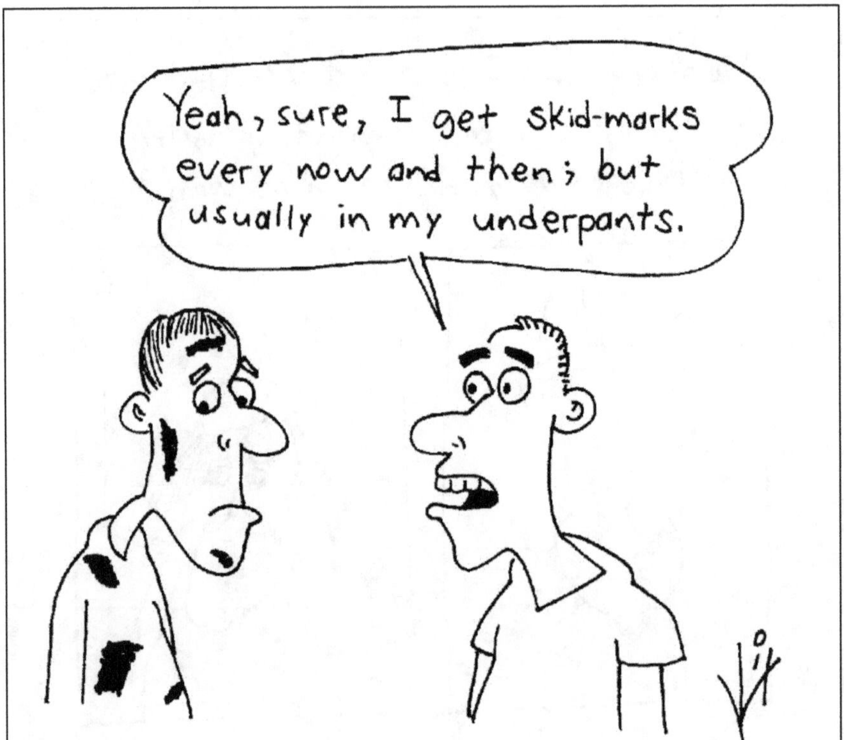
Yeah, sure, I get skid-marks every now and then; but usually in my underpants.

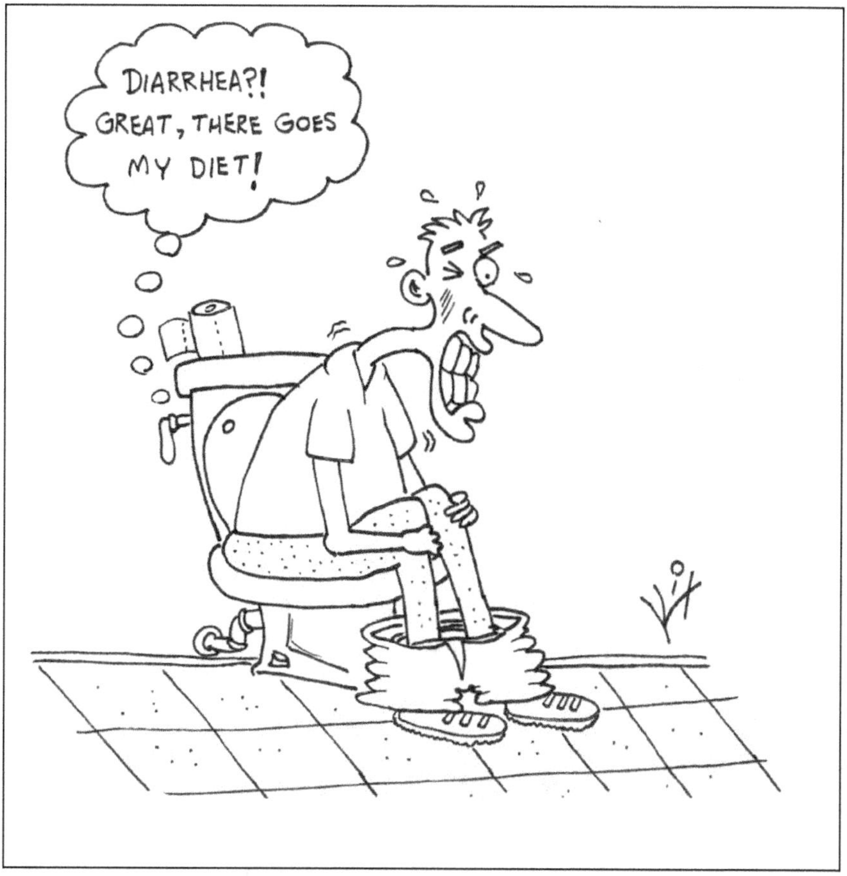
DIARRHEA?! GREAT, THERE GOES MY DIET!

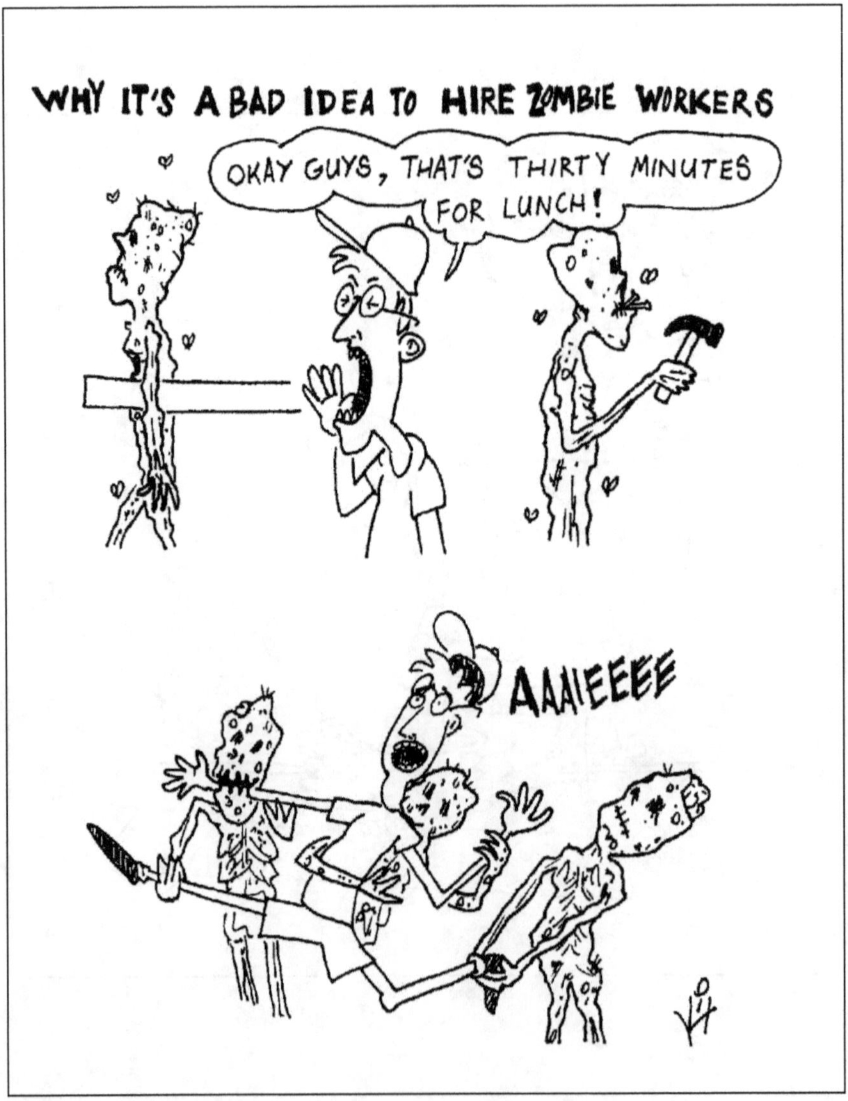
WHY IT'S A BAD IDEA TO HIRE ZOMBIE WORKERS
OKAY GUYS, THAT'S THIRTY MINUTES FOR LUNCH!
AAAIEEEE

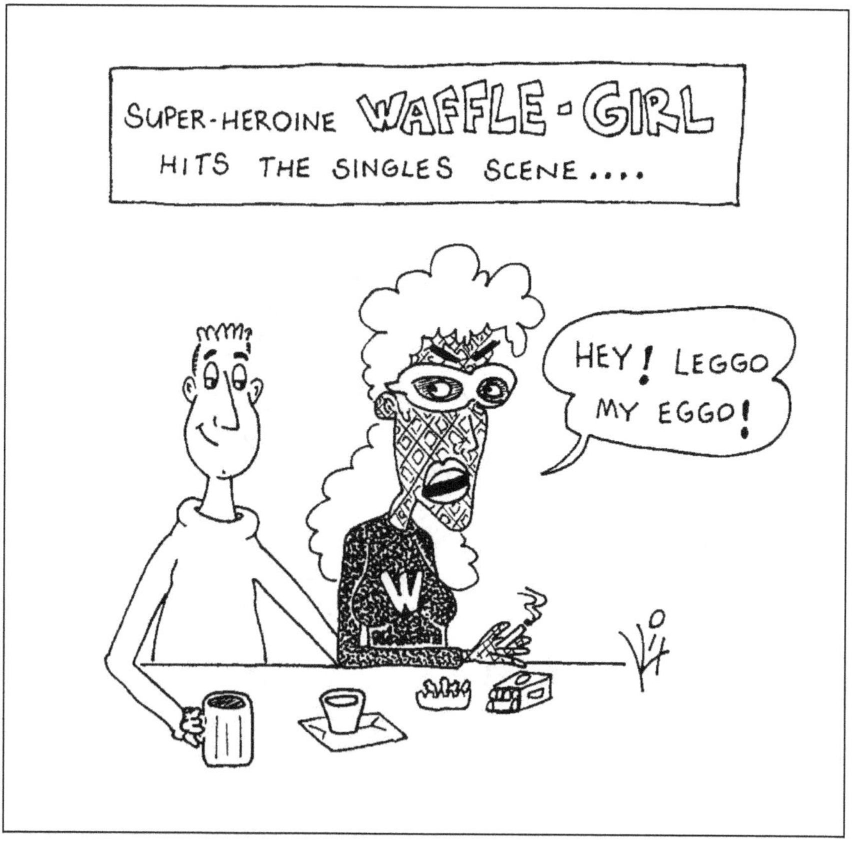
SUPER-HEROINE WAFFLE-GIRL
HITS THE SINGLES SCENE....
HEY! LEGGO MY EGGO!
W

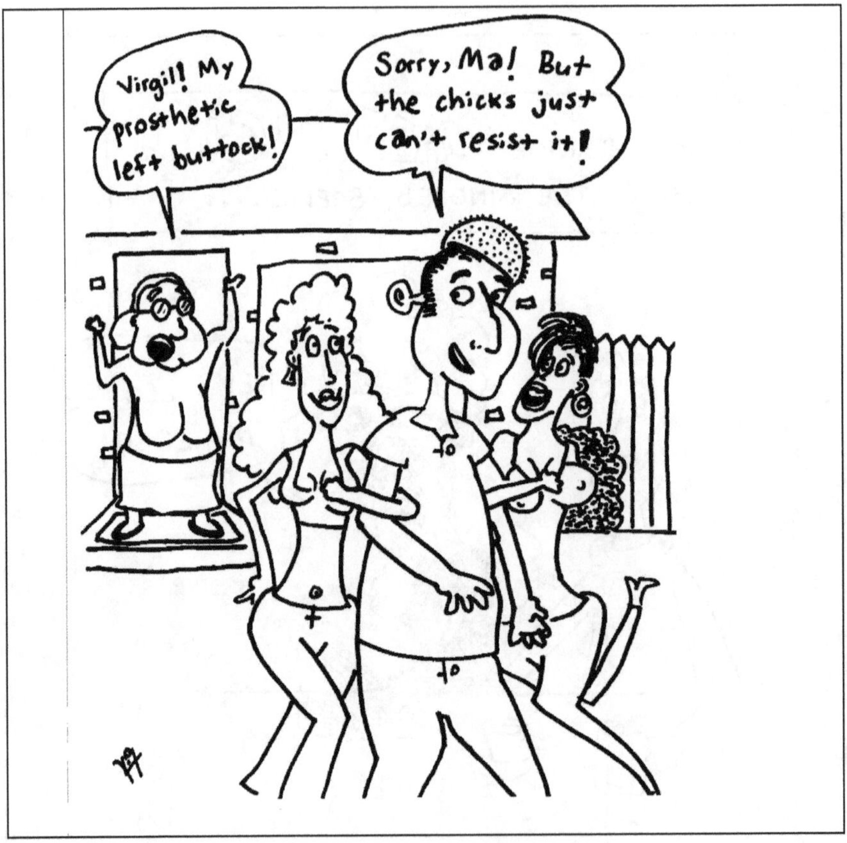
Virgil! My prosthetic left buttock!
Sorry, Ma! But the chicks just can't resist it!

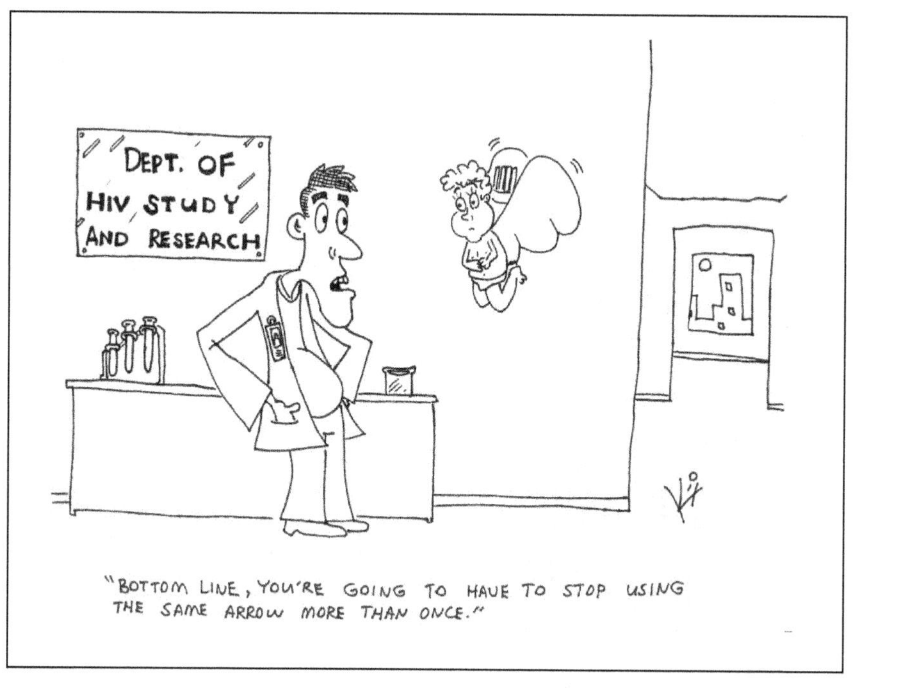
DEPT. OF
HIV STUDY
AND RESEARCH

"BOTTOM LINE, YOU'RE GOING TO HAVE TO STOP USING THE SAME ARROW MORE THAN ONCE."

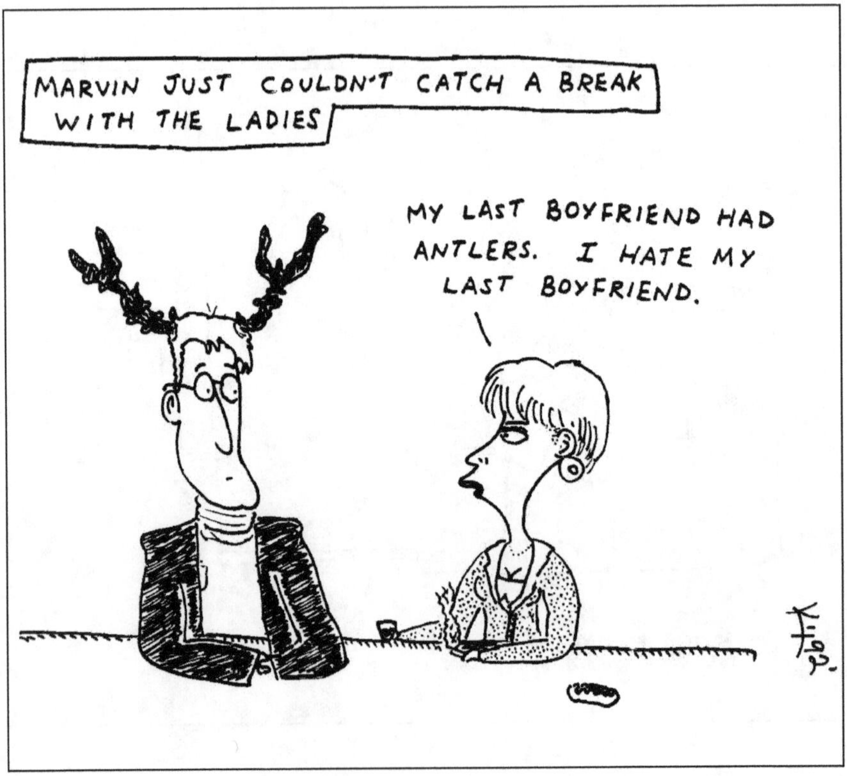
MARVIN JUST COULDN'T CATCH A BREAK WITH THE LADIES
MY LAST BOYFRIEND HAD ANTLERS. I HATE MY LAST BOYFRIEND.

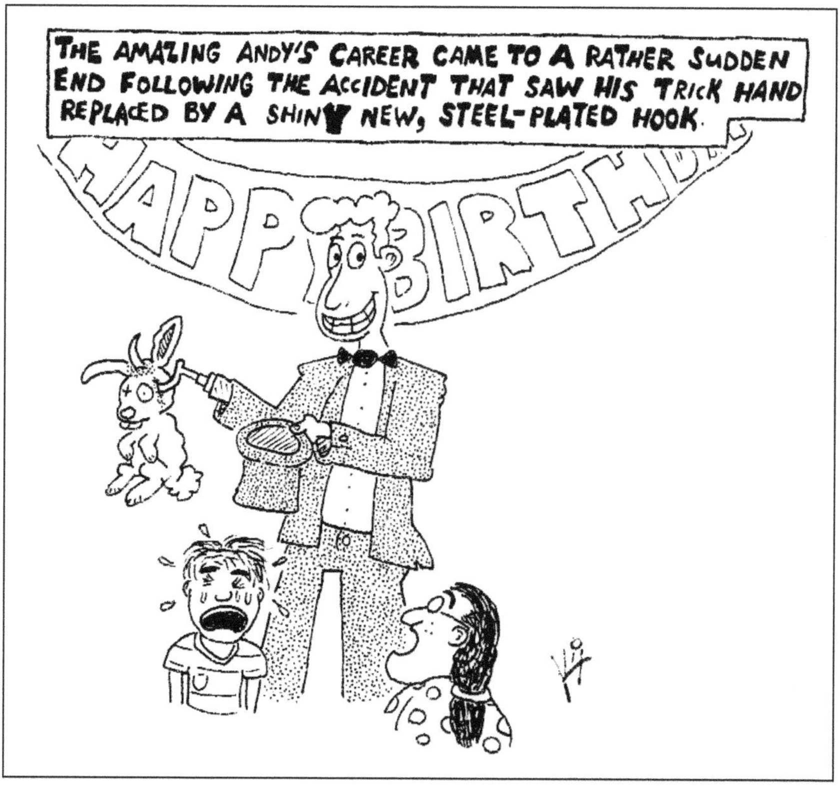
THE AMAZING ANDY'S CAREER CAME TO A RATHER SUDDEN END FOLLOWING THE ACCIDENT THAT SAW HIS TRICK HAND REPLACED BY A SHINY NEW, STEEL-PLATED HOOK.

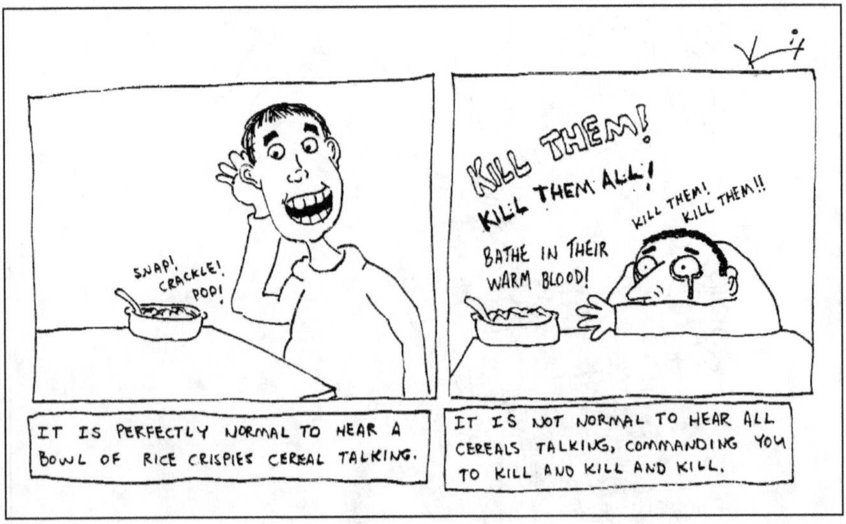
SNAP!
CRACKLE!
POP!
IT IS PERFECTLY NORMAL TO HEAR A BOWL OF RICE CRISPIES CEREAL TALKING.
KILL THEM!
KILL THEM ALL!
KILL THEM!
KILL THEM!!
BATHE IN THEIR WARM BLOOD!
IT IS NOT NORMAL TO HEAR ALL CEREALS TALKING, COMMANDING YOU TO KILL AND KILL AND KILL.

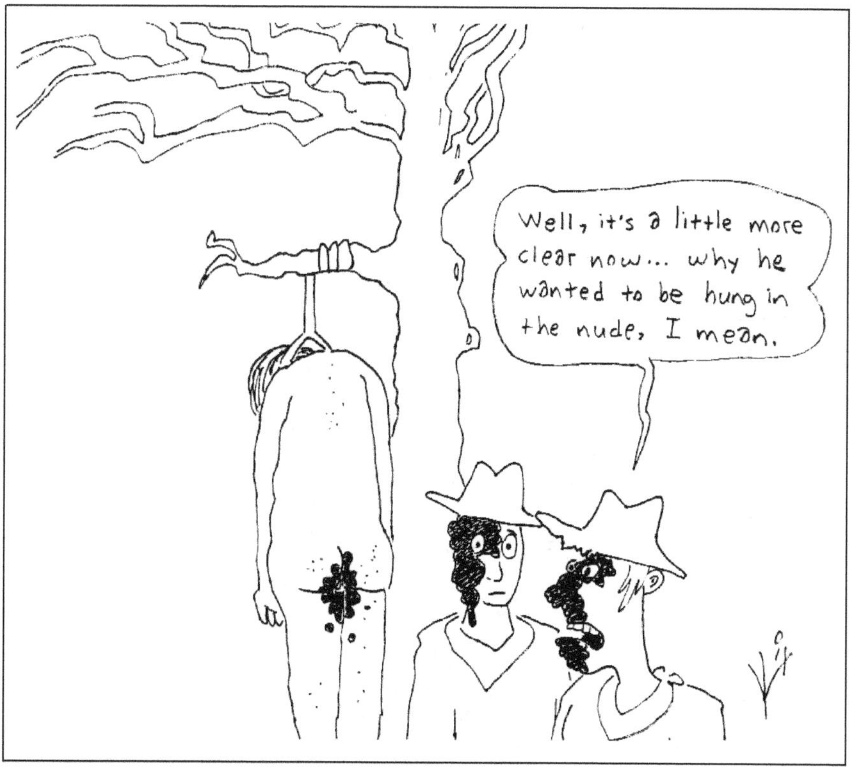
Well, it's a little more clear now... why he wanted to be hung in the nude, I mean.

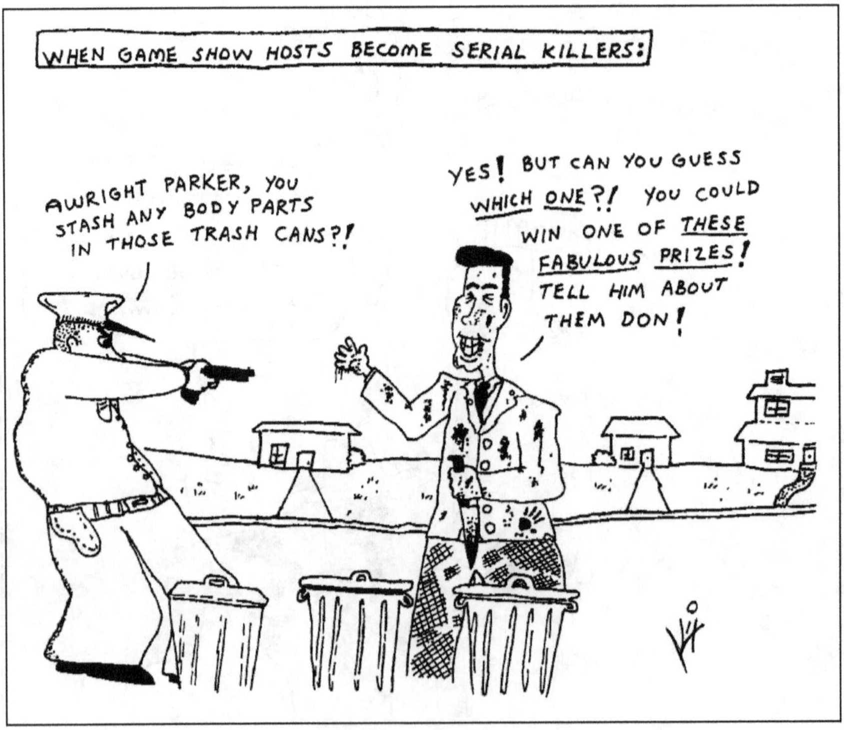
WHEN GAME SHOW HOSTS BECOME SERIAL KILLERS:
AWRIGHT PARKER, YOU STASH ANY BODY PARTS IN THOSE TRASH CANS?!
YES! BUT CAN YOU GUESS WHICH ONE?! YOU COULD WIN ONE OF THESE FABULOUS PRIZES! TELL HIM ABOUT THEM DON!

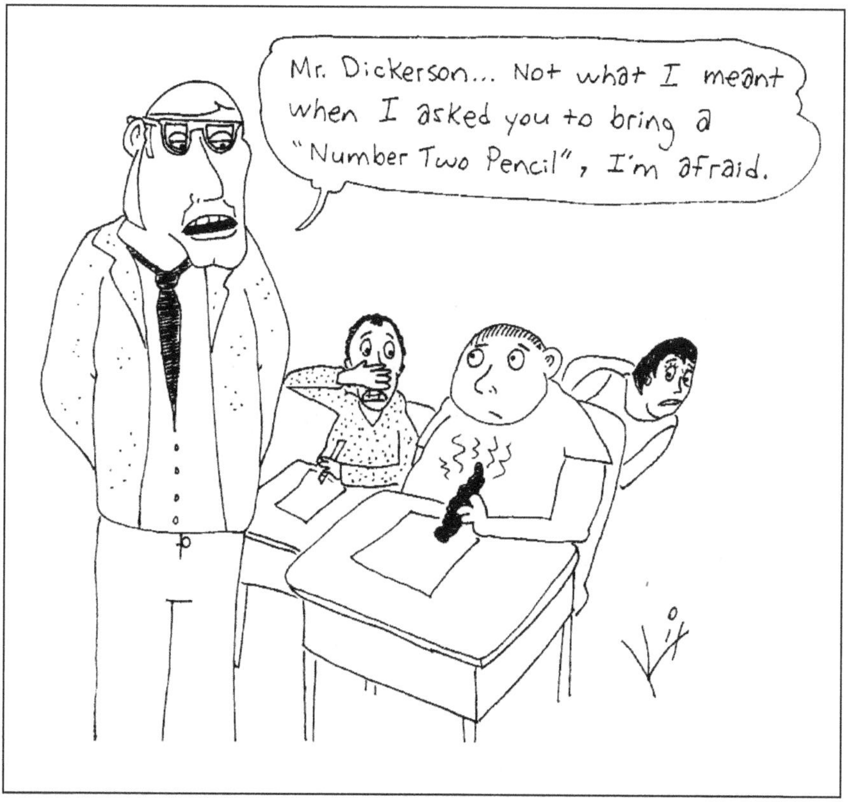
Mr. Dickerson... Not what I meant when I asked you to bring a "Number Two Pencil", I'm afraid.

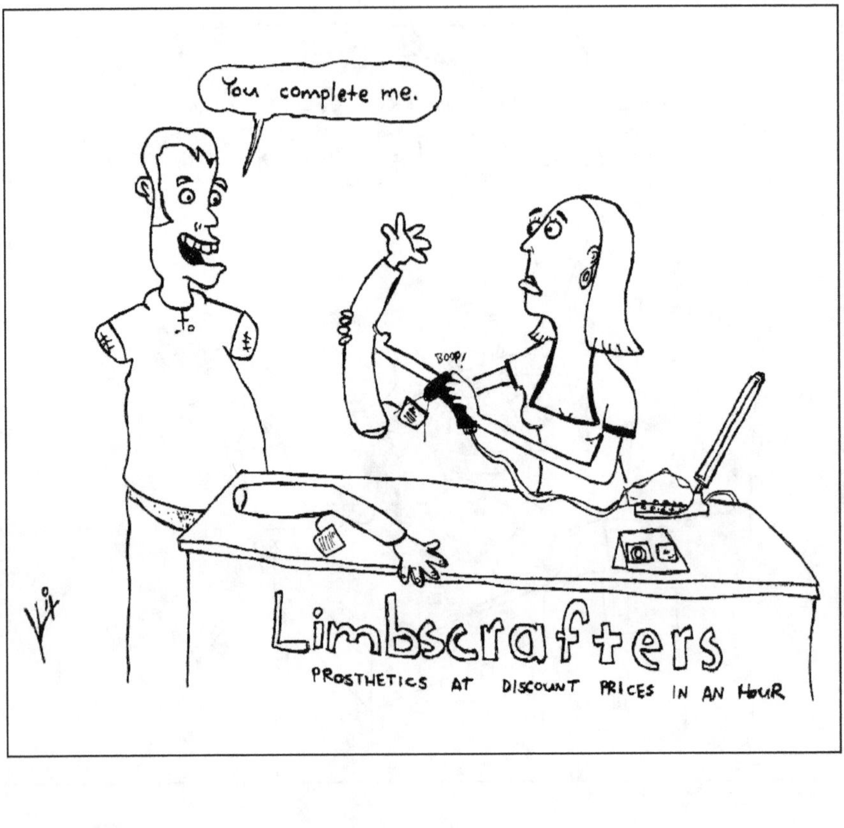
You complete me.
BOOP!
Limbscrafters
PROSTHETICS AT DISCOUNT PRICES IN AN HOUR

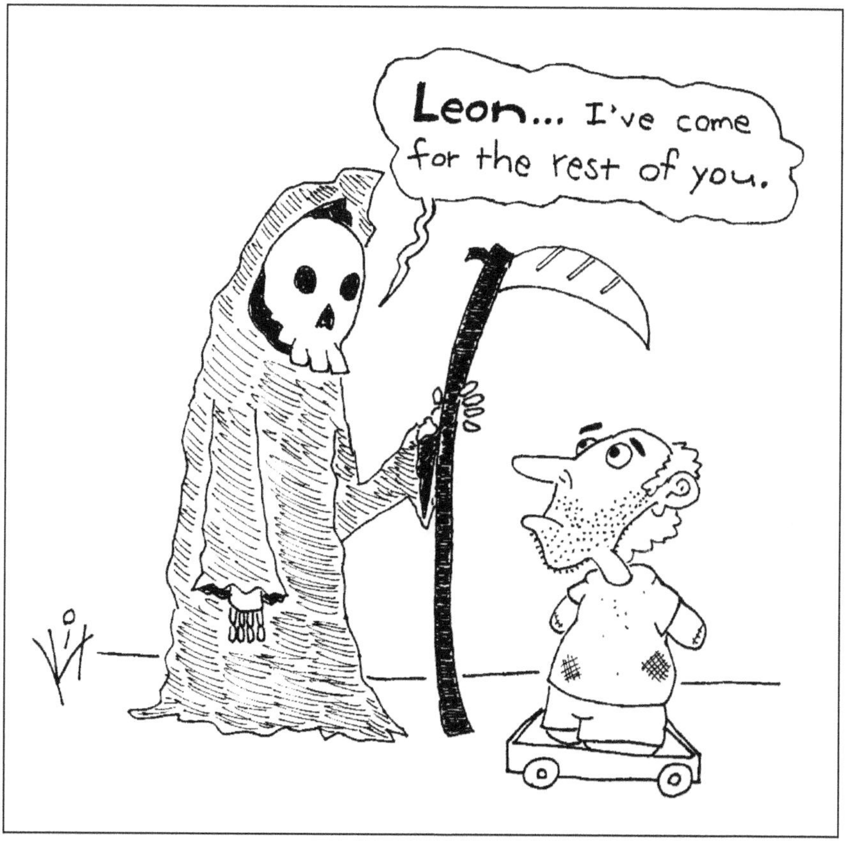
Leon... I've come for the rest of you.

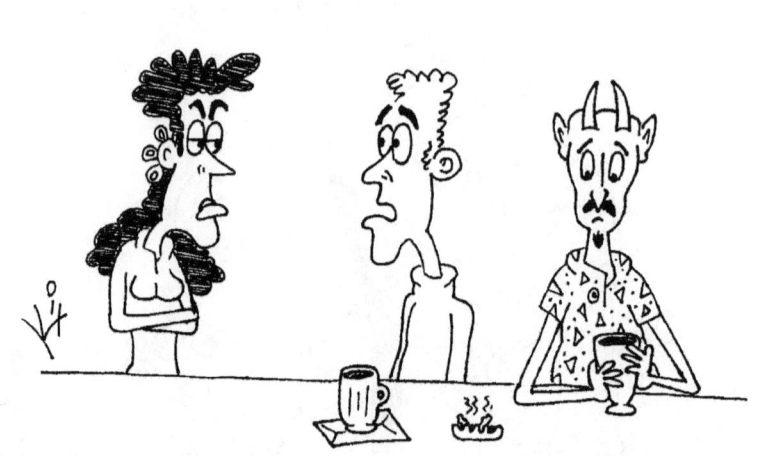

"Aw, c'mon Tara, just having a few beers with th' guy doesn't make me a 'Satan worshipper'".

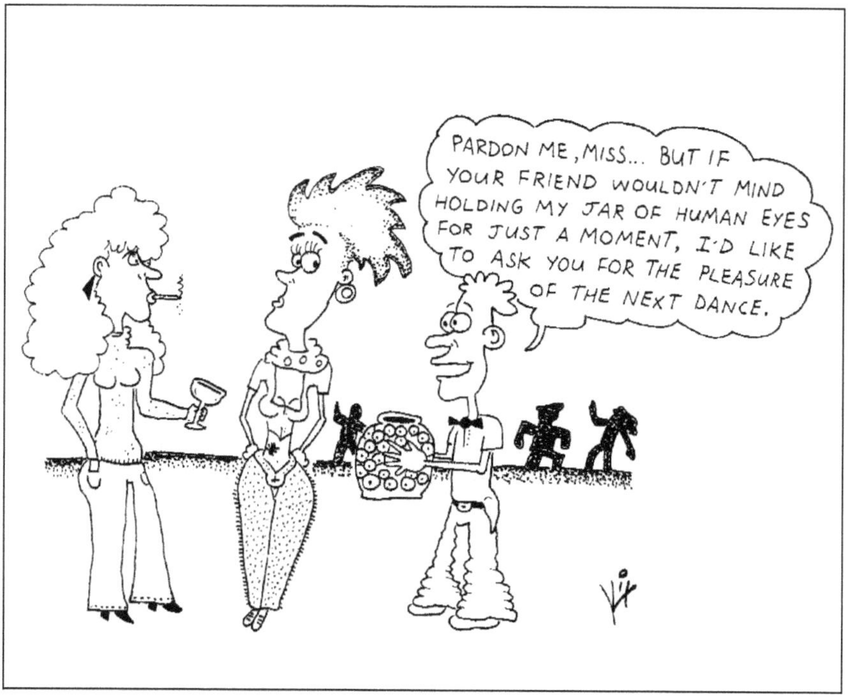
PARDON ME, MISS... BUT IF YOUR FRIEND WOULDN'T MIND HOLDING MY JAR OF HUMAN EYES FOR JUST A MOMENT, I'D LIKE TO ASK YOU FOR THE PLEASURE OF THE NEXT DANCE.

www.ingramcontent.com/pod-product-compliance
Lightning Source LLC
Chambersburg PA
CBHW051545170526
45165CB00002B/881
* 9 7 8 1 5 9 3 9 3 6 5 1 8 *